Governing With AI

Governing with AI

How the Public Sector Can Use Artificial Intelligence to Improve Performance

Mark Fagan and Ben Gillies

BLOOMSBURY ACADEMIC

NEW YORK · LONDON · OXFORD · NEW DELHI · SYDNEY

BLOOMSBURY ACADEMIC

Bloomsbury Publishing Inc, 1359 Broadway, 12th Floor, New York, NY 10018, USA
Bloomsbury Publishing Plc, 50 Bedford Square, London, WC1B 3DP, UK
Bloomsbury Publishing Ireland, 29 Earlsfort Terrace, Dublin 2, D02 AY28, Ireland

BLOOMSBURY, BLOOMSBURY ACADEMIC and the Diana logo are trademarks of
Bloomsbury Publishing Plc

First published in the United States of America 2026

Cover Design: Sally Rinehart
Cover Image © iStock.com/metamorworks

Library of Congress Cataloging-in-Publication Data Available

ISBN: HB: 979-8-2163-6932-5
         PB: 979-8-2163-6931-8
         ePDF: 979-8-2163-6934-9
         eBook: 979-8-2163-6933-2

Typeset by Deanta Global Publishing Services, Chennai, India
Printed and bound in the United States of America

For product safety related questions contact productsafety@bloomsbury.com.

To find out more about our authors and books visit www.bloomsbury.com and sign up
for our newsletters.

For Sandy and Meryle, Jamie and Cam, and Graeme
For three Fagans and a Moser

Contents

List of figures

Acknowledgments

The motivation for this book was to enhance the delivery of public services using artificial intelligence, tapping the potential and overcoming the peril.

We wish to thank Bailey Siber, Maximilian Bauer, Josh Sandler, and Darryl Slabe for their insights into the future of AI in government. We also thank Kate Victory Hannisian and Kimberly Lindberg for polishing our prose and figures.

A special thank you to Dan Levy and Lauren McHugh Olende. You have been our inspiration, sounding board, and source of expertise in this venture.

Introduction

If there is ever a time when you need government processes to go smoothly and without any hiccups, it's when it comes to getting your child healthy when she's sick. In the first few days after birth, a baby is vulnerable to a number of medical complications, and the last thing you would ever want as a new parent is to rush to the doctor with a sick child, in distress and panicked, only to find out your baby is not signed up for health insurance and is therefore not able to receive proper medical attention.

Unfortunately for many Ohio parents, this scenario used to be all too common. In 2011, Ohio had the eleventh-worst infant mortality rate in the United States (7.9 infant deaths per 1,000 live births, compared to the national average of 6.1),[1] and while the causes of this poor rate were many, one was the length of time it took to enroll children in a managed care plan or Medicaid. It took an average of seven to ten days to get babies signed up, meaning that if anything happened in those first few days of life, a distraught parent showing up with a sick kid had the devastating experience of not being able to easily access the critical help their child desperately needed.

In 2018, as part of a comprehensive bipartisan effort to reduce the number of heartbreaking outcomes, Ohio's Department of Administrative Services (DAS) turned to a new tool based on artificial intelligence (AI)—affectionately dubbed "Baby Bot"—for help. Previously, when a baby was born, a human caseworker would need to enter the newborn's information into their mother's Medicaid plan, which took time and resulted in errors. The AI-driven Baby Bot program instead received a child's information on the day the baby was born and automatically entered that information into their mother's file, checked for errors, and ensured the newborn was properly enrolled in Medicaid so they could start receiving the care they needed from day one—and they did all this within mere minutes. Moreover, Baby Bot was able to correspond with healthcare providers, only pulling in government caseworkers in situations when a complex scenario required human judgment—and the AI platform suggested possible remedies to the caseworker, who could then evaluate the options and make a final decision.

Thousands of precious staff hours were saved with caseworkers' attention reserved for only the most complex cases, errors were reduced, and citizens received better, faster service—with wait times for enrollment in healthcare coverage cut from seven days to just one.

This is the power and potential of artificial intelligence.

For a number of years now, the news has been filled with AI-focused headlines. Many are breathlessly optimistic—"New Study Shows Substantial Potential of Artificial Intelligence for the Swiss Economy,"[2] "AI Revolutionizes Ophthalmology with Oculomics for Cardiovascular Risk Assessment,"[3] and "Embracing AI's Transformative Power Has Massive Potential for Design and Construction."[4] Others are more cautious—"Ethical Concerns Mount as AI Takes Bigger Decision-making Role in More Industries,"[5] "Fake Photos of Pope Francis Go Viral, Highlighting the Peril of AI,"[6] and "The Promise and Peril of AI: Will Machines Make Us More or Less Human?"[7] But what seems understood is that AI is coming—and indeed, in many ways is already here—and will have far-reaching impacts on many parts of our lives.

For government officials sitting on the sidelines, trying to make sense of this entire AI ecosystem can feel overwhelming. Is "AI" the same as "machine learning" or "digital twins" (and do I know what either of those are)? Is using AI different than using big data? Is AI going to replace my team, or allow us to deal more effectively with a mounting workload? How can I know where to adopt AI into our processes? What can AI help with, and where might using AI lead to worse outcomes than having humans do a job; how can I evaluate the difference?

These are the questions we will answer with this book.

We know you, much like Ohio's DAS, want to serve your constituents well by providing better service even in a world of rapidly escalating costs. The evidence shows new technology can help with this goal. Already, examples abound of government officials using new tools to solve old problems while making their own working lives easier, and our goal is to show you how you can do the same. What's exciting is that given AI's far-reaching potential, it shouldn't matter whether you are in education, planning and transportation, healthcare, revenue services, safety, or just about any other government agency—you will likely be able to find help from AI tools.

This book is about helping you understand how AI can start working for you and your community, too.

Part I focuses on enabling you to lead a conversation about the use of AI in your organization. We begin with some context-setting, exploring the challenges and progress in providing quality public services efficiently with equity (Chapter 1). With this context, we then build the case for AI in delivering public services (Chapter 2). We then provide you in Chapter 3 with AI-101: What is AI? How does it work? When is it most effective? In Chapter 4, we focus on the potential risks and how they can be mitigated.

Part II details how to build the foundation for using AI in your organization. The starting point is establishing the policies, rules, and guardrails for using AI in the organization (Chapter 5), and ensuring you have the technological capacity to do so (Chapter 6). Next, we explore the expertise required to leverage AI, how those skills can be brought into the group, and the computing infrastructure necessary to support AI (Chapter 7). We conclude Part II with guidance on how to sell AI in your organization (Chapter 8), because buy-in up and down the organization is essential for a great AI plan to deliver value for constituents and your organization.

Part III is all about moving from talking about AI to doing AI. Chapter 9 provides a framework for you to identify and prioritize AI use cases for your organization. As an example of AI tools in practice, the application of the framework to the judicial courts is provided in Chapter 10. The final chapter offers a fast path forward using generative AI.

Each chapter begins with a summary of the content. Ben attended a seminar that emphasized how skimming text before a detailed read increases absorption of the material. He tried it and it worked, so we are adopting that approach in this book. We also provide a set of questions for you to think about as you read the chapter to help bring the generic text to life for your specific organization. The questions are repeated in the chapter with space for you to record your answers. We end each chapter with an assignment: Write the key insights you take from the text and how it is relevant to bringing AI into your organization.

Note that the content of this book builds on Mark's previous papers on artificial intelligence.[8]

Part I

Being Able to Lead the AI Conversation

Chapter 1: Delivering Public Services: Challenges and Progress

- Governments provide their constituents with a range of services, many of them critical to citizens' well-being, but face many challenges, including politics, complexity, resource access, and equity.

- To provide quality public services efficiently with equity, government agencies are acting along the four dimensions of service—policy, people, process, and plant/technology—and are often able to achieve substantial improvements in outcomes.

- Taking advantage of new technology like AI tools can often yield service levels approaching those of the private sector due to improved processing, streamlining, reliability, and other performance indicators.

Chapter 2: Building the Case for AI in Government

- Governments around the globe are using AI to improve the quality, efficiency, and equity of the services they provide to constituents. The applications are directly addressing the unique challenges of government service delivery.

- Initial efforts illustrate the power of AI to improve service delivery but also spotlight the risks and challenges of using AI.

- The risks of using AI are real and the cautions are important to understand. But the risks can be mitigated, enabling governments to tap the extensive benefits of AI for their constituents.

Chapter 3: Learning AI Basics: What It Is and How It Works

- AI has four characteristics: (1) the capacity to make decisions or support decision-making; (2) its decisions combine attributes of human intelligence; (3) it combines data sources and takes action based on the analysis; and (4) it exhibits continuous improvement.

- AI is an umbrella term for many different entities based on key characteristics like how the AI program learns, what tasks it is asked to do, and how it interacts with humans.

- While AI is not appropriate in all applications, in many circumstances, an AI tool can already do almost as good a job as a human but at a fraction of the cost or time needed, and there are some areas where AI is outperforming even top-rated human experts.

Chapter 4: Learning AI Basics: Risks and Mitigation

- Governments need to understand the risks associated with using AI so they can assess their impact and determine how they can be mitigated.

- The risks include data security, which can be minimized through anonymization and security protocols. Another risk is bias, which can be countered by using the full and representative dataset in training and using synthetic data to fill the holes. The AI hallucination risk can be overcome by verification.

- The broader list of risks includes disinformation and deepfakes as well as the impact on employment. For each concern, there are actions to reduce the risk, including clear guiding principles for adopting AI, ethics oversight boards and audits.

- Governments are in the driver's seat, with the ability to opt to use or not use AI. In some applications, the risk outweighs the benefits and alternatives to AI are the best path. If using AI, an agency decides how it will be used, what risks are acceptable, and what guardrails are put in place.

Chapter 1

Delivering Public Services
Challenges and Progress

Chapter Summary

Governments are responsible for providing a range of services to their constituents, many of which are critical to citizens' well-being. Unfortunately, the public service faces numerous challenges while doing so, related to politics, complexity, resource access, and equity. Recognizing the challenge, many government agencies across the United States and abroad are taking steps to overcome these issues. By acting along four dimensions of service—policy, people, process, and plant/technology—these agencies are frequently able to achieve substantial improvements in outcomes.

Policy reform ensures government work remains relevant and efficient, while examining processes can simplify and speed up approvals and outcomes for constituents. Investing in professional development of civil servants means educated, attentive, and engaged personnel working hard to provide the best possible assistance to citizens, and creating offices of innovation can break down silos and embed a culture of innovation into government processes across operations. Finally, taking advantage of new technology can often yield service levels approaching those of the private sector due to improved processing, streamlining, reliability, and other performance indicators.

Learning Questions and Food for Thought

1. What are some of the specific reasons government departments may struggle to provide quality service to their constituents?
2. Many citizens compare the services their government provides to the service they receive from private-sector companies. What are some differences between public and private entities that make it more difficult for a government to provide the same level of service as a private company?
3. Can you think of any examples within your own agency of changes you've made to address shortcomings in providing good service to your citizens?
4. What actions have you seen to improve service delivery within your organization (or inspiring initiatives done elsewhere)?
5. Within your own agency, are there dedicated programs for professional development to help upgrade the skills and education levels of public servants?
6. As a very visible example of using technology to improve service, how much did the US Postal Service increase its daily package sorting capacity when it invested in digital readers and automatic sorting machines in 2021?

Governments provide a wide array of critical services for their constituents. From roads and schools to public safety and healthcare, government agencies deliver the services we need. Since "We the People" pay for these services, government has an obligation to ensure quality, efficient, and equitable delivery.

Based on public opinion surveys, many citizens seem to think their government agencies are struggling to meet one or all of these obligations. In a 2024 Qualtrics survey, only sixty percent of respondents were satisfied with their state public services.[1] Federal government services fare better, but research by the American Customer Satisfaction Index finds that still not even seven in ten Americans are satisfied with services received at the national level.[2] When governments are unable to deliver on the promise of good service, the outcomes range from annoying to catastrophic. Take the case of North Carolina, where legislators have limited the number of employees their Department of Motor Vehicles (DMV) is permitted to hire. The agency has maintained almost the same staffing levels in 2024 as it had in 2004, despite state population growth of 2.3 million over that time, and can no longer keep up with such new demand. As a result, by 2024 residents needing to renew their driver's license were waiting up to four months for an available appointment.[3]

While this is a relatively minor inconvenience, one need only think back to the heart-wrenching images of starving New Orleans residents in the days after Hurricane Katrina to recognize the more devastating outcomes possible when government officials are unable to deliver on their promises—in that case, providing sufficient emergency food and water to those in need.

Challenges of Delighting Constituents

Governments face numerous challenges in delighting constituents with their delivery of services. Even just the first step of defining the "customer" is often difficult, as there are typically several. In providing mental health services, is the customer the direct recipient of the service? Their family? Civil society as a whole? All of the above? The answer impacts the definition of quality as well as the ability to be efficient and equitable with delivery. Then, we need to pile on expectations. Constituents often have unrealistic expectations of what government can deliver, and it doesn't help that sometimes politicians muddy the waters with pie-in-the-sky promises.

As you might have experienced yourself, constituents' perspectives around service quality are often set by what they see in the private sector where the customer is clearer, the recipient has choice, the "purchase" is unambiguous, and failure to meet expectations leads to bankruptcy. That mindset combines with compulsory taxation that funds government services to yield: "Darn it! I'm paying for these services . . . I expect better!" Let's look more closely at each of these six challenges: rule-based environment, limited resources, shifting priorities, lack of expertise, politics, and complexity of government.

> What are some of the reasons government departments may struggle to provide quality service to their constituents?
>
> ____
>
> ____
>
> ____
>
> ____
>
> ____

#1: Rule-Based Environment

Several constraints make fulfilling constituent expectations so difficult in the public sector. First, our governments operate in a rule-based environment. There are rules about procurement, budget, national security, and conflicts of interest, to name a few. Each rule has logic—accessibility requirements ensure the needs of users with disabilities are taken into account in the products and services the government buys, for example—but taken collectively the rules limit agency flexibility in knowing and meeting constituent expectations. As a result, it often leads to constituents feeling unsatisfied with the services they receive: "It's too slow." "The quality is poor." "Why do I have to wait so long?" "Why are my taxes so high?"

#2: Limited Resources

A second limitation is resource availability. Funds for services come from taxes. Raising taxes is extremely unpopular, even when the increases are targeted at corporations and/or wealthy individuals. The combination of constant tax rates and inflation leads to agencies needing to do more with less. A vivid example is funding the maintenance of the interstate highway system. In 1956, Washington established the highway trust fund to ensure money would be available to maintain the road system in the future. An 18.4-cent per gallon federal gas tax provides the funds. Over the intervening seven decades, the tax rate has not increased, while vehicle miles per gallon have gone up. The result is that for the last twenty years, fund revenues have fallen short of federal spending, requiring a money transfer from the US Treasury's general fund to make up the difference.[4] In 2024, that difference was over $18 billion.[5]

#3: Shifting Priorities

Beyond the absolute level of budget, how politicians and civil servants allocate funds varies depending on their priorities. Funds intended for education, transportation, and parks were diverted to healthcare during the Covid-19 pandemic. As administrations change, budget priorities also change. This makes multiyear projects difficult to pursue and often inhibits the adoption of information technology, which can take years to go from a request for bid until full implementation.

#4: Lack of Expertise

Governments often lack the expertise to adopt innovations that support quality, efficiency, and equity. Long and arduous hiring practices are one barrier. Another is compensation levels. According to the Congressional Budget Office, federal government employees with a bachelor's degree earn about ten percent less than their private-sector counterparts, and those with a professional degree or doctorate earn a whopping thirty percent less than those working for private companies.[6] The difference is similar among state and local government employees, who earn an average of 17.6 percent less than private-sector employees with similar education levels.[7] The differential is even larger for technical and managerial specialists.

One more factor is at play: risk aversion in the public sector. Innovation involves risk. Being in the public eye with news outlets on the prowl for "failure" stories, agencies exhibit an extreme case of loss aversion bias. Innovators want to live on the knife edge—succeed or fail fast and move on. Most government agencies prefer to be a follower, not a leader.

#5: Politics

Government service delivery is integrally linked to the political landscape. Priorities and resources are dictated by the political process, and the political challenge begins with the cut-the-budget mantra. Running for office often involves a pledge to reduce taxes. After the election this can translate into reducing agency budgets. Each administration brings its own agenda, leading to new priority organizations receiving funding and others losing budget. This budget whipsaw can limit service delivery investments, especially when trying to plan multiyear projects.

Many citizens compare the services their government provides to service they receive from private-sector companies. What are some differences between public and private entities that might make it more difficult for a government to provide the same level of service as a private-sector company?

#6: Complexity of Government

The size and scope of services governments must offer can hamper effective delivery. Every organization finds it difficult to do everything well, but the private sector can pick and choose its distinctive expertise, while constituents expect their government to be strong in all domains. There is also the challenge of coordination across separate government agencies. Silos occur for many reasons, such as system limitations, security concerns, or lack of mandates and resources to do so. As well, academics (such as Peters, 2018[8] and Christensen and Laegrid, 2015[9]) argue that the New Policy Management (NPM) approach that has become predominant in many governments across the country has exacerbated siloing, given NPM's strong focus on departmental targets and fragmentation over collective goals.

Another issue is working between levels of government. Federal rules can impact state and local service delivery in a number of ways, sometimes requiring states and cities or towns to take certain actions—often with an accompanying cost—or constraining what a local official can do, which can have wider-reaching implications. Take the case of the Verrazzano Narrows Bridge that connects Brooklyn and Staten Island in New York: Federal law stipulates the Metro Transit Authority can only collect tolls on the bridge from vehicles going onto Staten Island, not into Brooklyn. The MTA not only loses millions in toll revenues per year because of this limitation, it also "increases congestion in the Holland Tunnel under the Hudson River as motorists return to Staten Island through New Jersey to avoid payment of the toll."[10]

For a more far-reaching example impacting states across the country, in 2005 the federal government passed the Real ID Act that imposed minimum standards for anti-fraud security features into driver's licenses and mandated verification requirements when issuing these IDs. The cost to states of meeting these various obligations was over $11 billion.[11] The need for collaboration also extends to funding. Much of the money to build municipal water treatment plants comes from the federal government, passed to the states and then to the local water authority. Each level has its own rules and timelines. Consider the federal "Buy Made in America" requirements that limit the sources and materials used in federally funded infrastructure.

We share these constraints (summarized in Figure 1.1) not to depress you but to be sure you have a solid understanding of the world of government, how AI needs to fit into this fabric, and how AI can help overcome these challenges and improve government service delivery.

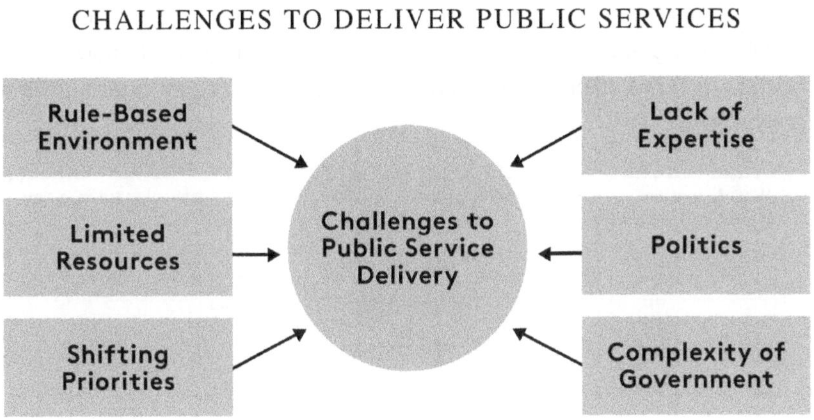

CHALLENGES TO DELIVER PUBLIC SERVICES

Figure 1.1 Challenge to deliver public services. Generated by the authors.

Government Improvement Actions

For many years, four simple letters—CEQA—struck fear into the hearts of developers on the West Coast. Short for the California Environmental Quality Act, this was a despised piece of legislation that outlined the requirements for local and state agencies to analyze and identify environmental impacts before approving projects. Protecting the environment is a critical responsibility of government, but the CEQA rules were so onerous that it took developers almost a decade to receive approval for their projects. Time is money, and the CEQA was costing them millions.

To their credit, state officials acknowledged this criticism and revised the act such that certain classes of project—like alterations to existing buildings or minor infill developments—are exempt from assessment as they do not have significant environmental impact, while larger projects such as mixed-use developments in transit priority areas similarly do not need to produce an impact assessment as long as they meet certain predefined criteria.[12] Moreover, the California Legislature also decreed that for work designated an "Environmental Leadership Development Project," judicial reviews and challenges are fast-tracked to a 270-day period, rather than following the conventional process that can take two years or more.[13] The result was a more efficient approval process that not only protected the environment but also helped developers build the critical housing and infrastructure Californians need, in just a fraction of the previous approval time.

This is just one example among thousands of policymakers across the country recognizing their own agency's shortcomings and making their operations more efficient, more cost-effective, and of better quality for their customers.

What actions have you seen to improve service delivery within your organization (or inspiring initiatives done elsewhere)?

Governments across the political spectrum are taking action to improve their outcomes, acting along four dimensions—policy, people, process, and plant/technology—to implement opportunities for change, and the results are often massive. In 2016, then-Governor Gina Raimondo implemented an executive order in Rhode Island that forced agencies to review their "policies" in order to remove outdated and onerous requirements, leverage national best practices, and align statutes with regulation and implementation.[14] At the beginning of the process, Rhode Island had 1,387 active executive branch agency regulations; by the end of the process, 467 of these were amended, 433 were consolidated into 134, and 160 were repealed.[15] As many regulations had been added to over time and therefore become quite bloated, officials could streamline many of them. For example, the state Division of Taxation merged over a dozen regulations about motor vehicle taxes into just one, and the Department of Health "cut the length of the implementation plan for its Special Supplemental Nutrition for Women, Infants, and Children (WIC) Program from 672 to 29 pages."[16]

Process reengineering is also improving public sector service delivery. In October 2024, for example, the New York state government passed a series of regulatory changes to make the process of opening a restaurant easier. Restaurateurs are now permitted to submit a full liquor application with their restaurant application, and are allowed to open with a temporary permit as they await final approval.[17] Earlier in the same year north of the border, the British Columbia provincial government in Canada launched a Building Permit Hub—a one-stop location that standardized the permitting application for the entire province.[18] As previous authorizations for homebuilding often required multiple applications to many different ministries related to issues such as riparian areas, water licenses, heritage inspections, and road rezonings, the new, single comprehensive application is designed to simplify work for applicants while simultaneously cutting processing and review times.[19]

Governments are also upgrading their workforce, the **people** who make things happen. Professional development programs are bringing leading-edge service delivery concepts, frameworks, and training to the public service. At the federal level, the US Office of Personnel Management (OPM) has worked with agencies across the US government on building current training programs and frameworks for future leaders. Dozens of departments have created their own internal training programs, all found in a single searchable database on the OPM's website (opm.gov). These in-house programs are often supplemented with opportunities to attend professional development programs at many of the nation's top universities.

The federal government has also been active in bringing new talent into its agencies through novel programs such as the Presidential Management Fellowship, which selects advanced degree holders (who do not work for the government) for positions within a number of government departments. The goal is to bring fresh ideas and expertise into the public service, and the two-year fellowships often lead to permanent employment for the fellows.

> Within your own agency, are there dedicated programs for professional development to help upgrade the skill and education levels of public servants?
>
> ____
> ____
> ____
> ____

Going beyond traditional mandated training, state governments large and small are similarly providing internal and external resources to their employees to improve their skill set. These include a partnership between New York State and its Civil Service Employees Association union that offers financial assistance to cover tuition fees, certifications, and exam costs for its members,[20] while the Missouri Leadership Academy graduates two cohorts of state leaders per year in a program focused on leadership, people management, and systems change.[21]

Beyond upskilling existing employees, governments are creating new departments to focus on innovation and effectiveness. The Mayor's Office of New Urban Mechanics in Boston, Massachusetts, was launched under Mayor Menino in 2010 to "encourage greater civic engagement in the city through the use of innovation and experimentation" because Mayor Menino believed the government was "too bureaucratic and lacked a human face."[22] The City of Chicago likewise created an innovation office to harness technology to "provide residents and City departments with user-friendly, accessible, innovative, and reliable digital services" while gathering and using data to share with residents and between departments to improve city decision-making and outcomes.[23] The department teaches officials in other agencies how to develop and use data to yield more positive outcomes. With their guidance, for instance, the mayor's office developed a novel racial equity impact assessment that helped determine where to build twenty-four new affordable housing projects.[24]

> As a very visible example of using technology to improve service, how much did the US Postal Service increase its daily package sorting capacity when it invested in digital readers and automatic sorting machines in 2021?
>
> ____
>
> ____

The idea of a dedicated innovation department has filtered up to higher levels of government as well, with dozens of states setting up such agencies with a range of objectives that can be quite broad—such as ensuring government products and services are "as effective, efficient, and responsive as possible" in New Jersey[25]—to more specific, such as Ohio's innovation office's mandate to improve user experience and incorporate technology and better streamlining into government services.

Finally, using new information technology to improve their **plants**, governments have made significant strides in the past decade. Examples abound, some of which improve back-end processes while others are far more visible to the public. While ordering a package online has become effortless for us as consumers in the internet era, have you ever stopped to think about the impact this massive new demand had on the US Postal Service? American parcel delivery doubled in under a decade, and the USPS could not rely on old practices to sort and deliver these products on time. In 2021, it invested in new digital address readers and automatic sorting machines to scan mail for destination information and efficiently send it to sorting facilities. Thanks to such automation, USPS doubled its daily package sorting capacity to 60 million between 2021 and 2023.[26]

The Department of Health in Florida invested in a new system to digitize files, streamline its documenting process, and create a central location to input and store sensitive information during the healthcare licensing process. The result was a reduction in processing times for healthcare licenses from six weeks down to just three days.[27]

Do you remember how difficult it was to get in touch with different government departments before the advent of the 311 phone system? It seems so dated now, but before 1996, you'd need to track down the number of the department you needed and call them directly to be redirected internally. But in that year, Maryland launched America's first 311 telephone system, which has made connecting with governments a relative breeze. Thirty years later, many municipalities are building on this one-stop approach to communication, upgrading to an online 311 platform where users can get help with graffiti removal, noise complaints, and parking enforcement while also reporting issues such as parking violations, looking up service requests, and making payments—all without having to spend time on hold or speaking with an agent. Similarly, many cities have moved from roadside parking meters to parking payment smartphone applications, allowing users to easily pay for parking from anywhere without having to run back to the meter, sometimes even enabling drivers to see available spaces nearby.

The improvements described above (and summarized in Figure 1.2) are helping to improve service delivery, but the citizenry is still expecting more. We believe that the next leap forward will come from the use of AI, which

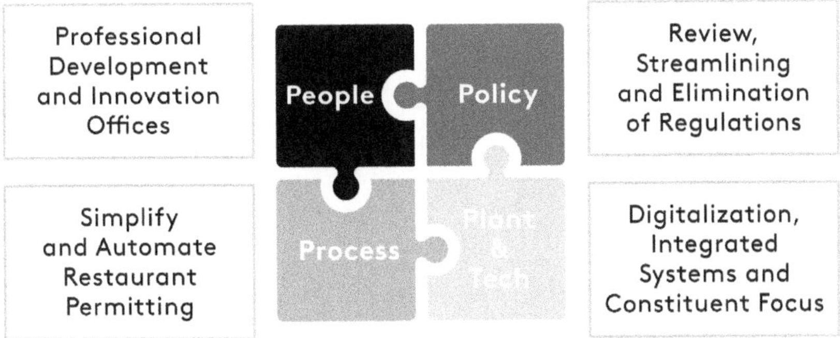

Figure 1.2 Service delivery improvement examples. Generated by the authors.

can broaden, deepen, and speed improvements. The remainder of the book provides you the background, concepts, frameworks, and tools to make that a reality in your organization.

> Write the key insights you take from the text and how it is relevant to bringing AI into your organization.
>
> ____
>
> ____
>
> ____
>
> ____
>
> ____
>
> ____
>
> ____

Chapter 2

Building the Case for AI in Government

Chapter Summary

Governments around the globe are using AI to improve the quality, efficiency, and equity of the services they provide to constituents. The applications are directly addressing the unique challenges of government service delivery. AI is being used to simplify the hiring process for agencies. It is also being used to eliminate repetitive and tedious work. On the constituent-facing side, AI is streamlining permit requests, providing 24/7 answers to questions in multiple languages, and reducing traffic congestion.

The results of initial AI efforts illustrate the power of AI to improve service delivery, but they also shine a light on the risks and challenges of bringing AI to bear. For instance, the datasets that AI tools rely on to make predictions are not in themselves neutral, so as AI learns, it can reinforce existing biases.

The bottom line: the cautions are important to understand, so enter the AI world with your eyes wide open. But the risks can be mitigated, enabling you to tap the extensive benefits of AI for your constituents.

Learning Questions and Food for Thought

1. What examples of AI have you seen in the private sector that could have value in your organization in serving constituents?
2. What are the pain points in your organization? Where might AI help?
3. What AI risks are you concerned about?

If you've picked up this book, you probably think artificial intelligence (AI) has a role to play in your own agency or department's operations. We agree. The proof is that millions of Americans—and people around the world—are already engaging with AI when they connect with their government. AI is becoming an important complement to the improvement actions we've described in the previous chapter. There are numerous examples of leveraging the power of AI to address the challenges of delivering public services. These are only examples to spark your thinking. The list of AI opportunities is much larger than what we can include here. However, there are also some cautions to be aware of—there is no free lunch!

The Power of AI for Government

Governments around the globe are using AI to improve the quality, efficiency, and equity of the services they provide to constituents. The applications are directly addressing the six unique challenges of government service delivery we explored in the previous chapter. Illustrative examples are detailed below.

> What examples of AI you have seen in the private sector that could have value in your organization in serving constituents?
>
> ____
> ____
> ____
> ____

#1: Rule-based Environment

In Vancouver, Canada, as in many North American cities, applying for a building permit was a complex process due to the number of regulations a developer needed to follow. From zoning and environmental regulations to street closures, companies looking to build had to submit many separate applications to over a dozen city departments. All these rules have their individual purpose, but collectively they add up to an onerous and costly process for anyone looking to add new housing and office space to the community.

To address this challenge, the local planning department launched an AI-based product called eComply that dramatically simplifies the process for developers. Rather than multiple applications, now they submit just one, and the eComply system reviews their application, including designs and drawings, and alerts applicants if the document is incomplete or the project will fail to meet regulations without having to wait for a manual review.[1] While this does not eliminate the rules they need to follow, it makes it much easier and faster to do things correctly and makes the process of submitting corrections much more efficient.

Meanwhile, as anyone who has applied for a government position knows, the process can be tedious for applicants and costly for agencies in order to follow all the policies around who and how to hire. AI facilitates hiring by using algorithms to sift through large numbers of applications and select profiles best matched for the position at hand. AI supports the hiring decision by analyzing potential for skills that the employee might not yet possess. In theory, this also introduces less bias into the hiring process compared to traditional procedures. However, many recent cases have found that bias embedded in AI systems through historical discrimination still leads to disproportionately low hiring of women and racial, socioeconomic, and other minorities, so there is much work to be done in improving these systems.[2] But as these tools improve, the vision is that they will make it easier to ensure departments are meeting commitments around hiring at much lower time and financial cost.

> **What are the pain points in your organization? How might AI help?**
>
> ____
>
> ____
>
> ____

While still in early stages, government officials already envision a world where AI helps them with their retrospective regulatory review and ensures a certain standardization to regulation development. This is thus far most advanced at the federal level, where the US Department of Health and Human Services, the Department of Transportation, and the Department of Defense have all been piloting AI tools. These tools analyze all department policies, highlighting areas where regulations may be redundant, outdated, or contradictory to one another so that these can be removed or modified as appropriate. As well, the tools take regulations that have been written by hundreds or even thousands of people over the years and provide them with a unified format and language.[3]

#2: Limited Resources

You've likely seen, and perhaps even clicked on, the "Chat with us" button in the bottom right-hand corner of a web page, only to be connected with an AI chatbot that can further direct your inquiry. These types of chatbots, computer systems that simulate human conversation, are a high-leverage tool to provide quality services efficiently and with equity 24/7 without needing to invest in a larger staff of human call center agents. The Rwandan government worked with Babylon Health to create chatbots capable of assisting the triage process for patients calling the hospital. Upon hearing the callers' symptoms, the triage tool provides recommendations for accessing care. In theory, this would help address minor medical concerns that would otherwise require waiting for a doctor's appointment and prioritizing those needing immediate care. As this was a pilot program, the AI only provided suggestions to nurses, who conveyed information back to patients; future iterations could remove the call center nurses altogether, enabling access to health care at a vast scale, and more efficient use of staff resources.[4]

Around the world, AI is also facilitating tax collection. The OECD in 2019 reported that more than forty tax authorities are using or plan to use AI.[5] For example, the Spanish government has teamed up with IBM's Watson to address questions about value added taxes. Since introducing Watson, the number of email inquiries to the tax authority has declined by 80 percent as Watson was able to answer citizens' questions.[6]

Moreover, AI can help ensure governments are getting the resources they are owed, being used to detect payment anomalies and fraud. Several countries use AI to predict bad debts and prioritize collections. The US Internal Revenue Service is introducing an AI chatbot that is able to help those behind on tax payments set up a payment plan.[7]

Finally, research is finding employers can see improved retention by using AI systems that provide human resources teams with information on employees at risk of leaving and providing recommendations to ensure retention, from skills or leadership training to higher wages. Governments can use these same systems to reduce turnover, saving money on investments made in their teams.

#3: Shifting Priorities

Sadly, in recent years the unhoused population in Los Angeles County, California, has been going up. Sitting at 53,000 in 2018, today it is over

75,000, and for every permanent housing unit in the area, there is demand for another four more.[8] This has left local officials grappling with perhaps the most vexing question in public policy: Who do you help first? Over the years, they have answered that question in different ways—sometimes focusing on those most likely to recover quickly and gain stability, for example, other times going with "first come, first served," or defaulting to a lottery because more complex assessments were too difficult.[9] On top of this, assessment processes around need are often very problematic, with caseworkers asking very personal questions around topics like trauma, abuse, alcohol and drug use to people they have only just met, leading to inaccurate responses.

Officials recognize that the ultimate solution is more housing, but in the meantime, they are using AI to build a more rational process for allocating housing to unhoused people. Los Angeles has worked with experts at the University of Southern California to build an assessment tool using machine learning. Their goal is to remove the bias, flaws, and changing priorities of previous approaches and focus on what studies suggest is the most effective approach: helping those most in need. Whereas research showed old tools had bias related to the inaccuracy of information and bad data inputs, the new machine learning algorithms focus on only the key pieces of information that must be assessed, correct for built-in bias, and refine themselves to ensure more accurate scoring. While this is still in its early days, the objective is to provide a cost-effective, reliable, lasting process for ensuring the county's extremely scarce housing resources are being used in a way that provides maximum public benefit.[10]

#4: Lack of Expertise

AI's ability to analyze large datasets can also help mitigate the challenge of government complexity and a lack of staff expertise. Still looking at housing in Los Angeles, the government adopted a tool built at UCLA that analyzes large pools of data to predict—with a high degree of accuracy—who is at risk of becoming homeless within the next twelve months.[11] Rather than waiting for Los Angelenos in need to approach them (many of whom would not even know what programs were available or where to start after they had lost their house), staff at the Los Angeles County Department of Health Services contact these citizens and proactively offer them support and financial resources to keep them in their homes and enable them to access medical and other forms of assistance.[12]

#5: Politics

Policymaking can be difficult because politicians and other stakeholders are not necessarily subject matter experts and instead see the world (logically) through their own lived experiences. We imagine you might know someone who makes decisions based on their personal reality even when that reality does not tell the whole story or may be unusual compared to the circumstances of most other constituents. To help provide decision-makers with context that might help them see problems in a new light, governments in places like Pinellas County, Florida, and Elk Grove, California, are using large datasets and AI analysis to understand how to determine what data to measure that gets to the heart of the challenge they want to solve. They have enlisted AI platforms to pull in data, not only information that they collect directly but also statistics from other sources like the US Census Bureau and the Bureau of Labor Statistics to provide a comprehensive, multifaceted understanding of quality of life within their communities and to compare the local community with jurisdictions across the country.[13]

Stakeholders in these jurisdictions are able to move away from decision-making based on pet issues or individualized experience and instead focus on what the data shows are real challenges in their communities, armed with an understanding of which data to monitor to see whether solutions are working.[14] Because these AI platforms make it easier to compile and analyze data from diverse sources, they make it easier for governments to move away from tracking outputs (e.g., number of police officers on the street) and towards monitoring outcomes (e.g., a rise or fall in crime rates), so policymakers can focus on what data shows is actually working rather than what might "feel" right or be based on policies that were less effective but more easily measured.[15]

#6: Complexity of Government

Remember Ohio's Baby Bot from the introduction? Baby Bot was just one of four new "bot" platforms the state deployed in 2018 and 2019 to improve various aspects of its welfare service delivery, which was a complex system that involved thousands of daily interactions between public officials, private insurers, and healthcare facilities. The Disability Onset Alert Bot scans disability information and ensures changes do not impact an individual's eligibility, flagging any concerns for caseworkers. Request Bot manages a

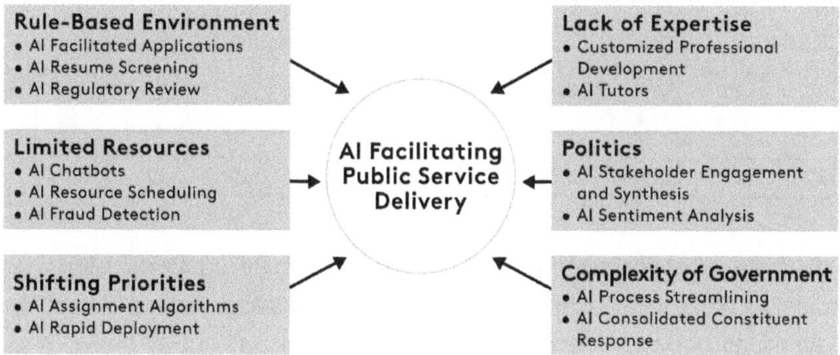

Figure 2.1 Examples of overcoming the service delivery challenges with AI. Generated by the authors.

self-service portal and sends information to users who request access to their case information. Finally, Pregnancy Bot builds on Baby Bot's success by notifying counties when Medicaid recipients become pregnant to ensure there is no gap in coverage for mother or child. These bots reduce inaccuracies, automate basic interactions between stakeholders, and do it all within minutes if not seconds, simplifying what can be complex processes for everyone involved.

Clearly, AI is here, not only in the private sector but in public agencies as well (see Figure 2.1). The challenge for government leadership is in how to leverage the benefits of AI while managing risk and doing so at scale. One of the most significant barriers to tapping the value of AI is a lack of understanding of AI in the government. Our goal in this book is to provide civil servants with the background they need to identify, prioritize, and implement AI where it generates a strong return on investment adjusted for risk.

The Rest of the Story

The results of initial AI efforts like the ones we've just described illustrate the power of AI to improve service delivery, but they also shine a light on the risks and challenges of bringing AI to bear. For instance, the datasets that AI tools rely on to make predictions are not in themselves neutral, so as AI learns, it can reinforce existing biases. Many states now use pretrial risk assessment tools to determine who should be granted bail, but academics have found evidence to show the data reflect racial and ethnic disparities, making the AI programs more likely to recommend incarceration for certain groups.[16]

What are the AI risks you worry about?

____

____

____

Bias is an often-mentioned challenge of AI, but as agencies begin to implement these tools, users are noticing other issues as well. Tens of millions of American baby boomers are in need of more assistance at home, and dozens of so-called "age tech" companies now exist that use AI to help look after older adults, and government agencies are exploring their potential. This technology includes motion sensors in a senior's residence that alert caregivers when the resident falls,[17] and wristbands that detect a user's normal activities (such as feeding themselves or tracking the number of daily bathroom visits) and warn an attendant when there is variation.[18] Yet these technologies have implications for the seniors under their watch. Researchers have found users often modify their behavior in an attempt to avoid causing an alert—they might try to avoid napping or will rush during their bathroom activities for fear these could send a notification to an attendant or, worse, their adult children.[19]

Moreover, some seniors' advocates worry that when families and caregivers start to use technology to check on their parents rather than visiting in person, the overreliance on AI tools may only exacerbate issues of senior isolation and loneliness.[20]

Finally, in their excitement to harness the power of this technology, policymakers might attempt to implement AI tools in inappropriate ways. In 2017, the US Department of Homeland Security explored a plan to use AI to determine whether an asylum seeker was likely to become a "positively contributing member of society" and whether they were likely to commit a terrorist act.[21] The project received serious pushback from AI experts who made a compelling case that computational methods would not be able to "provide reliable or objective assessments of the traits that [DHS] seeks to measure"[22] and that there is not enough data on events like terrorist attacks for an AI program to accurately predict the likelihood that a given individual is likely to commit one.[23]

While the DHS ultimately abandoned the idea, one can only imagine what kind of digital discrimination might have been baked into such an initiative, illustrating the risk of officials using poorly designed AI systems with potentially negative and serious implications for recipients of government services.

The Bottom Line

We care about you and your work. The cautions detailed above are important to understand. Enter the AI world with your eyes wide open. But the risks can be mitigated as detailed in Chapter 4, enabling you to tap the potential of AI for your constituents. For now, we turn to how exactly AI works, a critical foundation for understanding its application within your organization in the future.

Write the key insights you take from the chapter and how it is relevant to bringing AI into your organization.

____

____

____

____

Chapter 3

Learning AI Basics
What It Is and How It Works

Chapter Summary

There are four characteristics of artificial intelligence (AI): It must have the capacity to make decisions or support your decision-making; its decisions must have a combination of attributes of human intelligence (e.g., perception or reasoning); it needs to combine data sources and take action based on the analysis; and finally, it needs to exhibit continuous improvement. Early applications of AI focused on evaluating outcomes in games like chess. Today they have far more transformative applications, with autonomous vehicles being one of their most ambitious. Here a computer makes continual, split-second decisions to protect its own passengers and the people on the street and in surrounding cars.

AI is an umbrella term for many different entities based on key characteristics like how the AI program learns, what tasks it is asked to do, and how it interacts with humans. While AI is not appropriate in all applications, there are many circumstances where an AI tool can already do almost as good a job as a human but at a fraction of the cost or time needed, and even now, there are some areas—like searching and summarization or data analytics—where AI is outperforming even top-rated human experts.

Learning Questions and Food for Thought

1. Can you provide a definition of AI?
2. How do autonomous vehicles illustrate the core principles of AI?
3. What are the different types of AI that you can name, and can you explain what makes each one different?
4. What does LLM stand for, and do you know whether you've ever used an AI tool that employed an LLM?
5. Given the descriptions offered above, can you think of a simple tool that is theoretically possible with AI that could make your job easier and more efficient?
6. The US Postal Service was one of the first government agencies to develop an AI algorithm to help it improve its service. Can you guess what the algorithm did?
7. Given AI's strengths, what are some areas where it has a comparative advantage over humans?

In 2016 Mark learned about a new (and what he thought was crazy) innovation in the mobility space, a self-driving car. Entrepreneurs, engineers, software, and hardware experts came together to operationalize a computer-controlled car for everyday use. Mark later learned that the quest for autonomous vehicles (AVs) had begun decades earlier but really took root with the Defense Advanced Research Projects Agency (DARPA) Grand Challenge in 2003. The task was to have an autonomous vehicle traverse 142 miles in the Mojave Desert. None of the fifteen entries succeeded. But in subsequent challenges the technology improved dramatically, leading to cars rolling down the streets in many cities adorned with lidar (short for light detection and ranging), radar, cameras, and a very powerful computer.

Mark's first ride in an AV was in Providence, Rhode Island. The demonstrated project shuttle operated along a 5-mile loop from downtown to a transit desert community. Mark's impressions of the technology spanned the territory from awe to dismay. He was awed that the vehicle was able to operate at times without the safety driver's intervention. His dismay was triggered by the extensive time that the vehicle was operated by a human rather than a computer. Six years later, Mark was riding an AV taxi in San Francisco, there was no safety driver and the ride quality was as good as or better than when he drove.

AVs are a quintessential AI application. The computer completely replaces the human. As a human driver for over 50 years, Mark found himself amazed that his estimated 15,000 hours of driving can be codified into a series of 1s and 0s. Multiple AI technologies are integrated to provide a great ride. The ride begins with AI computer vision leveraging video, lidar, while radar and sound sensors are used to "see" what is happening in real time. Sensor fusion then integrates this information to provide a 3D picture of the operating environment with constant refreshing, just as your eyes and ears do when you are driving. Next, big data analytics use past experience to help predict what conditions will be encountered. Known as mapping, this process combines operating conditions across thousands of journeys to predict what the vehicle will encounter on a Saturday at 7:18 am on a sunny day in December when the temperature is 38 degrees versus a cloudy 30-degree day after overnight precipitation. Just as you know to watch out for black ice, the AV uses its history to prepare for slippery conditions.

AI behavior prediction algorithms are also in play. They are used to anticipate how others will act. Other cars, cyclists, and pedestrian behaviors must be reflected in the operation of the vehicle. Other AI systems convert the information into mechanical action. Increasing speed, decreasing speed, braking, turning on blinkers, etc. are all controlled by computer code. Other AI applications provide safety protocols, communications between the vehicle and a command center, and even honk the horn.

The AV example involves multiple, sophisticated AI systems working seamlessly in a high-risk environment. Other AI applications, such as searching for keywords in a bid document to provide office supplies, are much more straightforward. Both have broad applicability and value. Using them effectively requires a basic understanding of AI. That is the intent of this chapter.

Behind the Abbreviation—AI

Can you provide a definition of AI?

ATTRIBUTES OF AI VIS-À-VIS AUTONOMOUS VEHICLES

- **LIDAR, radar, video analyzed to see the environment, real time.**

- **Big data and edge computing to make decisions, continually.**

- **Robotics to initiate and complete physical actions.**

- **Data analytics to learn and improve.**

Figure 3.1 Attributes of AI vis-à-vis autonomous vehicles. Generated by the authors.

AI is defined by the Oxford English Dictionary as "the theory and development of computer systems able to perform tasks that normally require human intelligence, such as visual perception, speech recognition, decision-making, and translation between languages."[1] The operative word is intelligence, "the mental quality that consists of the abilities to learn from experience, adapt to new situations, understand and handle abstract concepts, and use knowledge to manipulate one's environment."[2]

There are four characteristics of AI. First, AI has the capacity to make decisions or at a minimum support your decision-making. Second, AI decisions require a combination of attributes of human intelligence from perception to problem-solving to reasoning to learning language.[3] Third, AI systems combine data sources and take action based on the analysis. This contrasts with preprogrammed responses.[4] Fourth, the decision-making provides feedback to the system for continual improvement.

Autonomous vehicles illustrate these characteristics (see Figure 3.1).

- Make Decisions: AVs are continuously making decisions, from pulling out into traffic after you enter the vehicle and moving along its route to stopping for red lights and pulling to the curb and letting you out.

- Requires Human Attributes: the AV must see, hear, and assess the behavior of others to make decisions.

- Combine Data and Action: the sensory information is processed and turned into action.

- Feedback and Improvement: the AV uses all of its experiences to continuously improve its understanding of the operating environment and decision-making.

> How do autonomous vehicles illustrate the core principles of AI?
>
> ____
> ____
> ____
> ____
> ____

Our understanding of what constitutes AI has evolved. Alan Turing, credited with the concept of thinking machines in the 1950s, established an AI threshold requirement that the computer be able to solve puzzles in a manner similar to humans.[5] Another view, articulated by John McCarthy, set the test as "getting a computer to do things which, when done by people, are said to involve intelligence."[6] Of course, involving intelligence is subject to debate.

Since Turing imagined AI, it has become reality by his definition. The early applications were playing games, checkers specifically. Success here led to an interest in seeing if a computer could beat a world chess champion. The theoretical answer was yes. The computer could evaluate all permutations of its own and the opponent's moves and devise a plan to win. For years the practical answer was no, since there was insufficient processing capacity to test all the alternatives. By the 1990s, the combination of greater computing capacity and increasingly efficient use of that capacity enabled IBM's Deep Blue computer to beat chess grandmaster Gary Kasparov in a dramatic 1997 showdown.

Yet another view of what constitutes AI comes from Darrell West of the Brookings Institution. He suggests AI requires three ingredients: intentionality, intelligence, and adaptability.[7] Intentionality refers to the intent of the human developing the AI to have the computer make decisions in the manner of a human. The AI algorithms that operate autonomous vehicles are designed to replicate and replace a human driver. West describes intelligence as using machine learning and data to make intelligent decisions. The autonomous vehicle must find and follow the best route to its destination while ensuring safety for its occupants and those in its path. At the core, the computer is determining how to incorporate multiple factors and make trade-offs. Adaptability refers to the ability of the computer to learn to adjust to new and ever-changing conditions. The autonomous vehicle is constantly gathering new information about its operating environment and adjusting its performance based on instantaneous changes in conditions.

The Many Flavors of AI

AI is an umbrella term. Under the umbrella, there are many different types of AI approaches and applications. We put ChatGPT to work unpacking AI into its segments. The segmentation is based on the following:

- Learning Paradigm
- Functionality and Purpose
- Techniques and Algorithms
- Application Domain
- Ethical Considerations
- Interaction Mode

While the list seems intimidating, the names are intuitive descriptions. A short description and example of each is provided below.

Learning Paradigm refers to how much training the model has to make its decisions. *Supervised learning* refers to models that learn from data labeled by humans. Input 1,000 images of cats and 1,000 images that are not cats but look like cats. Train the model to identify cats and then test to verify it is able to take new images of cats and identify them correctly. An offshoot of supervised models is self-supervised learning, where the model generates labels from the data itself. Unsupervised learning is where the model learns from unlabeled data by identifying patterns or structures. Pour out a bag of M&Ms and feed a picture of each into the AI model. It will observe the color difference between the candies and arrange them into groups based on color. You didn't train the model to organize the candies by color; it did so based on the pattern it observed. You can also add a layer of supervision by telling the model whether its work is what you expect.

> What are the different types of AI that you can name, and can you explain what makes each one different?
>
> ____
> ____
> ____
> ____
> ____

Functionality and Purpose address the breadth of the AI application. Narrower AI applications target a specific task. Image recognition to identify potholes on streets is one example. Another is algorithms that translate business license applications into multiple languages. A third is a chatbot that provides taxpayers with interactive, real-time questions and answers. Stronger applications enable the performance of multiple complex human tasks. AVs are in this category.

Technique and Algorithm: AI systems can also be categorized by the type of algorithm. There are *symbolic* or logic-based expert systems that use "if-then" logic to determine actions. An example is the evaluation of patents to assess their novelty. Another group is *statistical* AI programs. These programs use probability to address uncertainty in data to project outcomes. Predictive policing and natural disaster prediction are examples. *Machine learning* is where the algorithm learns to make predictions and decisions through examples, just as we do. A subset of machine learning is neural networks and deep learning. Here the goal is to structure the computer decision-making akin to the human brain operating at multiple levels at the same time. This is needed for complex problems such as AVs. A final group is *evolutional algorithms*, which rely on the concept of natural selection to solve problems. Examples include optimizing supply chains, searching for new drugs, and optimizing investment portfolios.

> What does LLM stand for, and do you know whether you've ever used an AI tool that employed an LLM?
> ____
> ____

The **Application Domain** segment consists of three primary approaches. First is *natural language processing* (NLP). The most common subset of these models is large language models (LLMs). ChatGPT, Claude, Bard, and other programs leverage NLP/LLMs to complete tasks. If you asked AI for help writing a poem for a friend's birthday, it was done by an NLP. The second approach is *computer vision* to identify and interpret images. The program that identified cat images was such a model. In the world of providing government services, computer vision is helpful in identifying environmental degradation, automating passport control, and detecting cancer. A third category is *robots*. That Roomba that vacuums your home is a common example. Governments are using robotics to inspect bridges using drones, handle bomb disposal, and dispense medications.

Another way to categorize AI regards its **Ethical Considerations.** *Explainable* models are intended to be interpretable by humans. Thus, the decision logic and how it plays out is understandable. <u>Fair</u> AI intends to make sure that the system is designed to minimize any bias across groups. <u>Safe</u> models are architected to provide reliability and certainty. This is essential for any program that creates a public safety risk, such as national security defense systems and, of course AVs.

The final segmentation grouping is around **Interaction Mode**. At one end of the spectrum is *human-in-the-loop*, where people provide feedback during the decision-making and/or learning process. At the other end of the spectrum are *autonomous* AI systems, where the models run independent of humans. Between these two ends are collaborative AI systems, where AI complements human decision-making. Think of this type of AI as your copilot.

How the AI "Magic" Is Made

For many years, Mark assessed the quality and efficiency of warehouses. How well was space utilized? Was it well organized? Was it safe for workers and secure for materials? He needed to answer these questions and a dozen more for multiple warehouses located across the country. Pre-AI, his approach was twofold. The gold standard was conducting on-site evaluations. The downside was the cost in time and travel expenses, especially since observations were needed every week or two. Where site visits were not practical, warehouse personnel took photos and sent them in. Mark evaluated them as best he could, but the assessment was quite limited.

> Given the descriptions offered above, can you think of a simple tool that is theoretically possible with AI that could make your job easier and more efficient?

Enter AI image recognition software trained on hundreds of good and poor warehouse images. The photos address specific concerns such as unsafe acts, crowded aisles, and unutilized space. We built a simple model using images and can have a platform like Clarifai search the images for concerns. It is not as good as the gold standard, but it is much more efficient than Mark manually looking at hundreds of images. With a modest additional investment in time and resources, an Occupational and Safety Health Administration (OSHA) inspector can build an algorithm that can use daily video footage of warehouse operations and automatically identify concerns about worker safety. Management can use the same information to assess product quality and worker productivity. The exception reporting algorithm completes the task in a fraction of the time it would take a person to do so and with better accuracy.

What makes the magic? It is not magic, rather, it is translating how a human learns and turning it into computer code. Think of an AI algorithm as a recipe. An experienced chef can make a perfect soufflé every time by following instructions that have been tested and refined over time and training again and again until the nuances are mastered. The same is true for how AI models can identify potholes in the road. The recipe is a set of instructions that tell the model what a pothole is and how to identify it. The more complex the task—such as identifying a pothole in the pavement versus one at a utility cover and only those that are more than five inches in diameter and greater than three inches deep—the more instructions are needed. But the approach is always the same. Just as the chef trains through trial and error, the AI system does the same. In the case of AI, the computer has the power to see patterns, learn from them, and improve on the initial "recipe." The more training, the better the outcome.

LLMs such as ChatGPT and Claude can write that beautiful birthday poem for your friend by predicting how words follow each other. We do it all the time. When someone starts a sentence, and we finish it, we are using our experience to predict what will be said. Fill in the blank: I need some eggs, so I am going to the ___________. Through experience, we know that the most likely answer is "store" or "grocery store." It could also be "to the chicken coop," but we have learned that unless you are on a farm, "coop" is not the answer. The LLM uses the same logic to build sentences. It considers the probability of the next word in a sentence and selects the highest-likelihood word. The sources of establishing the probabilities are everything on the internet, social media, books, and so on. Thus, the training base is huge and therefore, the LLM has the context to know the answer to an egg query is store not coop. AI is driven by statistics, not magic.

How do you build a computer program that is more cost effective and higher quality than yourself? The generic process for developing and utilizing

RECIPE FOR MAKING THE MAGIC

1. Define AI's goal
2. Collect the training data
3. Select model "flavor"
4. Teach the model how to "think"
5. Confirm model outcomes
6. Put the model to work
7. Confirm the model's value

Figure 3.2 Recipe for making the magic. Generated by the authors.

an AI program consists of the following seven steps and is summarized in Figure 3.2:

- Define the problem: What is the AI intended to accomplish?

- Collect and clean the data: What data are available to train the model? Make sure it is clean, unbiased, and not in violation of copyright.

- Choose an algorithm: What "flavor" model is the best fit to solve the problem?

- Train the algorithm: combine the model logic and data to teach the model how to "think."

- Test and improve the model: confirm the model provides rational outcomes. If not, understand why.

- Deploy the model: put the model to work solving the problem.

- Monitor and improve the algorithm: confirm the model does solve the problem; continually look for opportunities to refine the outcome.

> The US Postal Service was one of the first government agencies to develop an AI algorithm to help it improve its service. Can you guess what the algorithm did?
>
> ____
>
> ____

One of the earliest AI algorithms was developed by the US Post Office to read handwritten zip codes on letters. ChatGPT details the following example of teaching an AI model to identify handwritten digits.

- *Step 1: Define the Problem: Create an AI that can recognize numbers (0–9) written by hand. This is helpful for scanning checks, forms, or quizzes.*

- *Step 2: Collect and Prepare Data: Use a dataset like the MNIST dataset, which has thousands of images of handwritten numbers. Prepare the data by resizing the images to be the same size (28x28 pixels) and converting them to grayscale (black and white) for simplicity.*

- *Step 3: Choose an Algorithm: Use a type of neural network called a Convolutional Neural Network (CNN), which is great at recognizing images.*

- *Step 4: Train the Algorithm: Feed the AI thousands of images of handwritten numbers, along with their labels (e.g., "This is a 3"). The AI learns by adjusting itself to correctly match the image with the right number.*

- *Step 5: Test the Algorithm: Show the AI new images it hasn't seen before and check if it predicts the numbers correctly. For example, provide an image of a handwritten "5" and see if it recognizes it as a "5."*

- *Step 6: Evaluate and Improve: Determine the level of accuracy needed. Then measure accuracy (e.g., "It got 95 percent of the numbers right"). If it's not accurate enough, try using more data or adding more layers to the neural network.*

- *Step 7: Deploy the Algorithm: Integrate the model into an app or scanner to automatically read handwritten forms.*

- *Step 8: Monitor and Update: If people write numbers in new styles, update the AI with more examples to help it improve.*

<table>
<tr><td>Given AI's strengths, what are some areas where it has a comparative advantage over humans?

</td></tr>
</table>

The foregoing are examples where AI adds significant value all center on the power of image recognition algorithms. This is just one area where AI has a comparative advantage. Other areas where AI can complement humans are:

- Searching, finding, reading, and summarizing information: Need a one-page summary of that proposed legislation? AI is ready to deliver.

- Writing prose: A retirement party roast? AI will do it in twenty seconds.

- Interactively answering questions: Tired of constituents asking what day is trash pickup after a holiday? A chatbot eliminates the time and aggravation of responding to repetitive questions.

- Pattern and anomaly recognition: Trying to find tax evaders? AI can identify fraud.

- Sensing emotions: Not sure if you are reading body language correctly at zoning board meetings? Do some training with an AI algorithm.

- Integrating multiple inputs and projecting outcomes: Head hurting from trying to determine the best budget allocation based on constituent interests, department needs and revenue projections? AI is better than aspirin.

A full description of each step and associated examples are provided in Chapter 9. While AI is good at many tasks, however, it does not offer a panacea for policymakers. It is critical to also understand some of the challenges with this new technology, a topic we explore in the next chapter.

Write the key insights you take from the chapter and how it is relevant to bringing AI into your organization.

Chapter 4

AI Basics
Risks and Mitigation

Chapter Summary

AI offers the ability for government organizations to improve the quality and efficiency of their service delivery. However, there are risks associated with using AI that you should understand so you can assess their impact and determine how they can be mitigated. The risks begin with data security, protecting constituent-specific information. Here anonymization and security protocols minimize the concern. Nevertheless, there may be some applications where the risk outweighs the benefits and alternatives to AI are the best path.

The risk that garners the most attention is bias. If the data used to train the AI model are biased, then the outcomes generated by the model will likely be as well. The bias may result from missing data or historic discrimination that leads to models assuming the past should be perpetuated. This concern is mitigated by ensuring the full and representative dataset is used for training. Synthetic data, computer-generated information that mimics data in the real world, can be used to fill the holes.

You have probably encountered a third risk, hallucinations, a polite way of saying that AI programs can make up information and present it as fact. Recall that a LLM AI algorithm is using probabilities to build content, very unhuman. The key to overcoming hallucinations is verification. The good news is over the past year, LLMs have been getting more "real."

The broader list of risks extends to disinformation and deepfakes as well as the impact on employment. For each concern there are actions to reduce the risk, including clear guiding principles for adopting AI, ethics oversight boards and audits. At the end of the day, you are in the driver's seat. You can opt to use or not use AI. And if you are using AI, you decide how it will be used, what risks are acceptable, and what guardrails are put in place.

> ## Learning Questions and Food for Thought
>
> 1. What are the risks that would keep you from adopting specific AI applications?
> 2. What are applications where the risks can be effectively mitigated?
> 3. How do you think about the job impacts of AI?
> 4. What actions could you take to increase the trustworthiness of AI in your community?

"I love the idea of using AI to identify patterns in water usage so we can better predict requirements for potable water and know the amount of wastewater we need to process. I would also like to use AI to identify illegal taps. But I cannot use resident information for fear of a data breach." This city manager raises one of the most common concerns about AI, ensuring data security of the very information needed to train the algorithm. This is one of many risks in adopting AI in the public sector (see Figure 4.1).

Another is the risk of making biased decisions. Headlines including "Amazon Scraps Secret AI Recruiting Tool that Showed Bias Against Women"[1] are emblematic. If the training data is flawed, such as not having comprehensive information, the outcome will be as well. Abraham Wald provides a powerful, non-AI example of understating the impact of missing data.[2] Wald was in the US Strategic Statistical Group in the Second World War. One of his tasks was to determine where aircraft should be reinforced to reduce the risk of being shot down. He was presented with data showing the bullet holes on aircraft returning from missions. The bulk of the holes were in the fuselage, with comparatively few at the engines. The first thought was that the fuselage was the place for reinforcement, not the engines. But Wald asked a simple question: Where were the bullet holes on the planes that did not return, the ones shot down? The answer: they were hit in the engines. Thus, the missing data was the key to improvement (more reinforcement around the engines). If your dataset is missing information about the planes that did not return to base, you make incorrect decisions.

Returning to AI, a specific concern is that AI decision-making perpetuates historic biases. Consider this all-too-realistic scenario. Venture capital firms have a long history of hiring staff from elite business schools. The hires tend to be finance majors, which is a disproportionate male concentration. One of the firms decides to build an AI tool to help identify the best applicants

AI RISKS AND RESPONSES

Figure 4.1 AI risks and responses. Generated by the authors.

based on their top analysts. They rank order their hires over the last decade based on their comparative success. They then feed the résumés of the best performers into an LLM and train the model to evaluate the resumes of recruits and identify the most promising. It turns out one of the attributes of the top performers is playing a contact sport in college and another is being male. When the LLM is evaluating women's resumes, it is much less likely to see evidence of involvement in contact sports and will not see "male" and therefore discard women from consideration.[3] The AI is simply perpetuating the past, not finding the best applicants because it doesn't use Wald's insight and recognize what it is missing.

Another example of bias is in the public safety realm. AI predictive policing algorithms are often based on arrest data. But the chances of being arrested if someone is Black are twice that of someone who is white. Department of Justice data shows that "a black person is five times as likely to be stopped without just cause as a white person."[4] The data associated with arrests—socioeconomics, education, zip codes—are used to predict who will offend in the future. This information in turn is used to intensively police those environments, leading to more arrests and a vicious cycle that is perpetuated and strengthened by the algorithms. Ironically, race is not used in the algorithms, but the other attributes are surrogates for race.

Overcoming the Wald problem begins with understanding the problem and recognizing the lack of data representation. Next, the training data set can be curated in an effort to make sure all groups' information is included. If the data are insufficient, they can be augmented, and synthetic data can be generated. Data augmentation is enhancing existing data. For images, this might include changing the contrast level or changing perspective and scale. Text augmentation could include changing word order or synonym replacement. Synthetic data is computer-generated data that has the attributes of the underrepresented population. Thus, the missing data is added to the training dataset.

A third concern is the <u>reliability of the technology</u>. Returning to AVs, these vehicles have a harder time seeing dark-skinned people at night. A study published by Georgia Institute of Technology reveals that AVs are 5 percent less likely to detect a dark-skinned person than a light-skinned person.[5] This racial bias is not intentional. Rather it is a function of the technology and how it is deployed. Understanding the problem allows for solutions. Proposals include "specific post-processing image editing techniques to adjust contrast and brightness of captured input images, such as increasing brightness and contrast levels to dynamically counterbalance existing bias towards children and female pedestrians in low-brightness and low-contrast conditions."[6] Another is "penalizing overly confident predictions in low-contrast or low-brightness conditions, encouraging it to treat predictions more cautiously in these scenarios."[7]

A fourth concern is <u>hallucinations,</u> a polite way of saying that AI programs can make up information and present it as fact. An example that received much press attention was a legal brief filed by attorneys to a federal court judge in New York. The judge read the brief and was surprised to see cases cited that he was unfamiliar with. It turns out the lawyers used ChatGPT to write the brief. The algorithm "created" cases that sounded right but were in fact fake. The judge ordered the attorney to come to court and "explain why they shouldn't face sanctions for citing 'non-existent cases.'"[8]

The key to overcoming hallucinations is verification. Mark was looking for examples of companies that had redesigned their supply chains to source from countries that were nearer to the United States and had favorable geopolitical relationships with the United States. ChatGPT had many examples and the level of detail in the descriptions made them sound like they were real. He also asked for citations, knowing how the LLM generated the examples. The citations passed a sensibility test because they referenced real journals, author names, page numbers, etc. But when he looked up the citations, most were nonexistent. The good news is that over the past year, LLMs are getting more "real." However, the bottom line remains "use but verify."

Looking more holistically at the risks, there are national-level risks and application-level risks.[9] At the national level, the risks include societal risks such as disinformation, excessive surveillance, and even autonomous weapons. Economic risks such as job impacts, inequality, and expanding the wealth divide also sit at the national level. The overarching concern is that of ethics; are the specific uses of AI consistent with the values and norms of society?

> What are the risks that would keep you from adopting specific AI applications?

The application-level risks begin with basic security of the algorithm and preventing cyberattacks. There are also control risks, preventing a rogue placement of an AI app in less-secure systems. Moreover, as the algorithms self-learn and adapt, there is less human control and oversight of how decision-making takes place. This is the so-called black box problem: not even the original programmer knows the exact piece(s) of data the computer is basing its decision on. The most direct risk at the application level is that the algorithm generates poor and/or biased decisions.

Some risks exist at both the national and application levels. "Deepfakes," modifications of data and images that generate credible synthetic outcomes that did not happen, occur at both levels. To understand deepfakes, think about Photoshop on steroids. Trivial deepfakes abound on social media, where users make jokes or post videos of people performing dances while wearing the digitally superimposed face of a celebrity or politician. More serious dangers also exist. Audio technology was used to dupe a corporation into sending 200,000 British pounds to a foreign bank account by impersonating the voice of its CEO.[10] The impacts of disinformation range from undermining trust in corporations and government to reshaping social norms.

> What are applications where the risks can be effectively mitigated?

What About Jobs?

Whether you are a city manager, state director of public safety, or federal agency leader, AI also brings the challenge of managing your workforce.

First, you need to address change management as AI applications are implemented. This is covered in Chapter 8. Second, you must grapple with job eliminations. Autonomous buses mean the regional transit agency needs fewer bus drivers. AI chatbots eliminate the need for constituent services positions. While the need for fewer jobs has the benefit of requiring less budgetary funding, the challenge becomes what happens to the individuals whose positions are eliminated.

MIT's research effort on the impacts of AI on work offers the following insight: "Recent fears about AI leading to mass unemployment are unlikely to be realized. Instead, we believe that—like all previous labor-saving technologies—AI will enable new industries to emerge, creating more new jobs than are lost to the technology. But we see a significant need for governments and other parts of society to help smooth this transition, especially for the individuals whose old jobs are disrupted and who cannot easily find new ones."[11] The long-term approach is to orient education in schools and universities to prepare future workers to be AI-enabled. The short-term solutions center on retraining, which requires the combined efforts of employers, government, and worker organizations.

For you, the manager who needs to tell a fifteen-year employee they are being replaced by an AI algorithm, the challenge is very emotional. Mark and Ben have faced the challenge of replacing employees with technology, and it is really hard. Ben owns a small coffee shop and has been working to incorporate more automation in the production of lattes, cappuccinos, and other drinks. It has taken a long time to get buy-in from the baristas, but by using an incremental approach where the shop added one new tool at a time, the staff were able to react and see how these resources reduced injuries (e.g.,by eliminating many physically demanding repetitive motions), and above all, gave the staff more time to do what they love best—connect and engage with their customers. This was effective at winning their buy-in to change. We offer suggestions on how to manage this in Chapter 8.

How do you think about the job impacts of AI?

The AI Benefit—Cost Analysis, a Pragmatic View

Here is our dilemma: AI provides significant benefits but also introduces risks. Our job is finding the right balance between the benefits and costs. Mark has collaborated with a national court system to navigate the trade-off. The result is a pragmatic approach leveraging where AI's comparative advantages are high and the risks are limited.

AI can be used to support the administrative and substantive aspects of the courts. On the administrative side, AI can enhance decision-making for (1) managing the workforce; (2) operating the courts; and (3) managing evidence/documents/digital content. Scheduling courtrooms based on AI insights on the time it will take for a trial and predictive building maintenance are examples where meaningful benefits are achievable with little downside risk.

At the other end of the spectrum is using AI to support judicial decisions including (1) research; (2) analysis; and (3) decision-making. In the substantive arena, AI can find patterns of jurisprudence, summarize case facts, help draft opinions, and support decisions on probation, bail, or even sentencing. In the substantive domain there is more risk, but it is along a spectrum from minimal (finding key facts in hundreds of pages of documents) to extensive (where AI is predicting the flight risk of a criminal defendant).

A pragmatic approach to prioritizing the use of AI in the courts is to map the benefits versus the risks (think a 2 × 2 matrix) and prioritize the high-benefits, low-risk uses. Administrative functions including workforce scheduling, language translation, and screening resumes meet these requirements. These are the first use cases for implementation. Next, turn to low-risk substantive opportunities. Here, uses include searching for facts in documents, summarizing documents, and drafting boilerplate text. The basic idea is to crawl in order to walk, then walk. Running is after you have developed distinctive expertise, and then technology is even better.

Mitigating the Risks via Public Policy

Relying on industry to mitigate technical risks may not be enough because industry has mixed incentives. Risk reduction enables the continued growth of AI use, but investing in risk mitigation can be a drag on profits. While we can hope that the AI industry will err on the side of greater risk reduction, that is far from a guarantee. Enter government policymakers, who must walk the fine line of allowing AI applications that create private and public value while regulating the technology, especially to avoid bias and discrimination. Creating value without bias and discrimination is referred to as "responsible AI."

The starting point for responsible AI is establishing guiding principles for the development and use of AI. The OECD established a value-based set of principles for AI implementation, including fairness, transparency and explainability, security and safety, and accountability. Their recommendations "aim to foster innovation and trust in AI by promoting responsible stewardship of trustworthy AI while ensuring respect for human rights and democratic values."[12] Their proposals are intended to work in concert with other regulations covering data privacy and digital security. The OECD also provides guidance for policymakers, recommending they foster an AI ecosystem, build human capacity, address labor market disruptions and build trustworthiness at the international level.

The US National Artificial Intelligence Initiative Office suggests improving AI trustworthiness "requires a multifaceted approach, including R&D investments addressing key technical challenges, development of metrics, standards, and assessment tools to measure and evaluate AI trustworthiness, engagement in the development of AI technical standards, governance approaches for the use of AI in the public and private sectors"[13] The Biden Administration provided direction for federal agencies in achieving trustworthiness in the government's use of AI. This guidance recommends: (1) it should be performance driven where the benefits outweigh the costs; (2) the use cases should be directly tied to the training data and the data should be reliable and unbiased; (3) the results should be understandable to subject matter experts, well-documented and traceable; and (4) the use should also be monitored over time.[14] The Trump Administration rescinded the Biden guidance opting to focus on the United States as an AI development leader. "The United States must act decisively to retain leadership in AI and enhance our economic and national security. Today's executive order: Revokes the Biden AI Executive Order which hampered the private sector's ability to innovate in AI by imposing government control over AI development and deployment."[15]

AI Ethics Oversight boards or committees are tools for building trustworthy AI applications. An AI ethics committee serves as the organization's watchdog to ensure that the inputs, programming, and outputs of AI systems developed in the organization or purchased through third parties systematically and comprehensively meet the organization's core values. Staffing of the board should include subject matter and ethics experts, regulatory lawyers, and those responsible for the organization's strategy. The team should also include AI bias scouts who can identify vulnerabilities early on in the development stage.[16] Some companies have also deployed AI "champions" to serve as contact points between the board and regular employees.[17] Decision-making authority is key. If the board says an algorithm must be changed, it must be changed.

Northeastern University has created an AI ethics advisory board to support organizations that do not have the capacity to provide their own AI oversight.[18] The board has more than forty members drawn from multiple disciplines and sectors. It is also intentionally broad. The role of the board is strictly advisory: "The main goal of the board is to have the opportunity to [ask] the right questions and get the right answers. And then they're on their own."[19]

Another tool to operationalize the principles and recommendations described above is the AI audit. Audits provide an independent assessment of the AI algorithm. Does it do what it is intended to do? Are the data unbiased? Are the risks mitigated? An auditor's affirmative answers to these questions are trust builders. The audit process is nontrivial. "AI systems are not simply a few lines of code, but complex sociotechnical systems consisting of a mixture of technical choices and social practices."[20] The challenge is sufficiently complex that Stanford University's Institute for Human-Centered Artificial Intelligence ran a competition to find enhanced audit solutions.

The current state of the art focuses on evaluating the four stages of the AI lifecycle—design, development, deployment, and monitoring. In the design phase, make sure the goals, context, and assumptions are well defined. They should be pressure tested against the organization's values and norms. The development portion of the audit centers on the technical aspects of the model. This is also where the data are reviewed to ensure they are comprehensive, accurate, unbiased, and relevant to the context. During deployment, the audit evaluates if the intended goals are achieved, and if anomalies occur, they are researched and resolved. After deployment, regular audits function to continually monitor the AI decisions.[21]

The US Government Accountability Office (GAO) issued audit guidance for federal agencies in 2021. Their report provides a checklist and details for ensuring the integrity of governance, data, performance, and monitoring. In the high-risk data domain, the GAO recommends documentation of data sources, testing the reliability of the data, assessing the variables used in the model, and assessing the use of augmented (computer-generated) data.

The recommendations for performance include well-defined performance metrics, component and system-level testing, as well as whether the outputs are appropriate for the given context.[22]

The audit solution is great in concept but less robust in practice. The concern is that audits give the imprimatur of trustworthiness but with limited standards to guide the audit and auditors, "audit-washing" could result. The German Marshall Fund describes the concern:

> The risk is significant that inadequate audits will obscure problems with algorithmic systems and create a permission structure around poorly designed or implemented AI. A poorly designed or executed audit is at best meaningless and at worst even excuses harms that the audits claim to mitigate. Inadequate audits or those without clear standards provide false assurance of compliance with norms and laws, "audit washing" problematic or illegal practices.[23]

As mentioned above, they are also immensely resource intensive and may be difficult for smaller, newer companies to conduct.

To address this issue, ISACA (formerly the Information Systems Audit and Control Association) is a global community with a focus on increasing the trustworthiness of technology in general and AI in particular, and offers an AI Fundamentals Certificate. It covers (1) AI principles, concepts, and uses; (2) risks and ethical requirements; and (3) essential software and algorithms for AI applications and possibilities.[24] They have also published a manual for auditing artificial intelligence.[25] This is a start—but only a start. For audits to generate meaningful trust, they must be standardized, certified, and enforced. The financial auditing structure offers a helpful analogy. Figure 4.2 summarizes the various ways to build trust in AI.

What actions could you take to increase the trustworthiness of AI in your community?

____
____
____
____

You Call the Shots

At the end of the day, you are in the driver's seat. You can opt to use or not use AI. And if you are using AI, you decide how it will be used, what risks

AI TRUST BUILDERS

Fairness	**Privacy**	**Accountability**
Reliability	**Ethical**	**Fairness**
Transparency	**Oversight**	**Sustainable**

Figure 4.2 AI trust builders. Generated by the authors

are acceptable, and what guardrails are put in place. Guidance on how to bring AI into your organization is explored in greater depth in Chapter 7. Next, however, we'll focus on laying the foundation for using AI in your organization. Given the challenges we just outlined, we start with establishing the policies and processes (Chapter 5) and technology infrastructure (Chapter 6) that will guide the way you adopt, use, and monitor AI to provide services to your constituents.

<table>
<tr><td>Write the key insights you take from the chapter and how it is relevant to bringing AI into your organization.

____

____

____

____</td></tr>
</table>

Part II

Laying the Foundation for AI in Your Organization

Chapter 5: Establishing the Rules of the Game

- AI systems require a strong foundation of policies to provide governance and ethical guidelines, processes that define implementation strategies, and technology infrastructure—all of these guide AI adoption, use, and monitoring.

- A robust AI policy framework includes guiding principles such as fairness, transparency, and human oversight. Governance structures help ensure accountability, while compliance with legal and regulatory requirements prevents misuse.

- Procurement policies must account for ethical AI considerations, including bias mitigation and security measures. Ethical guidelines dictate human involvement in AI decisions and emphasize transparency in AI-driven outcomes. Continuous monitoring, evaluation, and incident management ensure AI remains effective and trustworthy over time.

Chapter 6: AI Technology Foundation

- Successful implementation of AI requires that an organization has the necessary technological capacity, including robust data infrastructure, computing power, and security.

- Ultimately, responsible AI deployment hinges on thoughtful policy development, careful implementation, and ongoing oversight.

- Balancing technological advancement with ethical considerations allows governments to harness AI's power while maintaining public trust.

Chapter 7: Developing Necessary Expertise and Infrastructure

- Successful AI adoption requires a combination of traditional skills (understanding regulations and comfort with making ethical decisions) and AI-specific skills (technical expertise on machine learning, data science, systems integration, and cybersecurity).

- A key requirement is comfort operating under uncertainty—in other words, being able to quickly absorb information, chart a path, and execute it.

- An organizational expertise assessment will identify the strengths and gaps of a team. Options for filling gaps include an AI training program, learning from the AI community, hiring consultants, and hiring staff.

Chapter 8: Selling AI to the Organization

- Buy-in up and down the organization is essential for a great AI plan to deliver value for constituents and your organization.

- Beyond using basic persuasion skills, selling the idea of bringing AI into an organization rests upon three principles of change management—change is an unnatural act, change management is a process, and "crawl, walk, run."

- Use one of the many frameworks for accomplishing change management and involve those impacted by AI initiatives in the design, development, implementation, and evaluation of the system. Start small and demonstrate that the change is done in bite-sized chunks. Provide a clear road map, simple steps, and sufficient resources to get the job done right.

Chapter 5

Establishing the Rules of the Game

Chapter Summary

AI systems require a strong foundation, consisting of the policies, processes, and technology infrastructure that guide AI adoption, use, and monitoring. Policies provide governance and ethical guidelines, processes define implementation strategies, and technology ensures the necessary infrastructure is in place. A robust AI policy framework includes guiding principles such as fairness, transparency, and human oversight. Governance structures, like AI oversight committees, help ensure accountability, while compliance with legal and regulatory requirements prevents misuse. Several jurisdictions, such as Massachusetts and New York City, have implemented AI policies to promote transparency and mitigate risks.

Procurement policies must account for ethical AI considerations, including bias mitigation and security measures. Ethical guidelines dictate human involvement in AI decisions and emphasize transparency in AI-driven outcomes. Continuous monitoring, evaluation, and incident management ensure AI remains effective and trustworthy over time.

Learning Questions and Food for Thought

1. What are some of the key elements that should be included in an AI policy document?
2. If your government or department establishes an AI steering committee, who should be a part of it?
3. Do you know which laws at the federal, state, or local level would govern or impact your ability to use AI tools within your organization?
4. How do you think AI procurement policies might differ from any existing policies your organization has in place? How might they be similar?
5. Are you familiar with your current incident management plans and policies; if so, what elements do you think can be repurposed for AI applications?

AI is like a house. The rooms are the different applications. The kitchen might be the restaurant licensing board chatbot. The living room might be the AI-optimized school assignments algorithm. The bedrooms could be the AI recruiting application, proactive building maintenance models, and AI-driven traffic flow software. Just as your physical house sits on a solid foundation of wood, stone, concrete, or steel, the AI house also needs to sit on a solid foundation. In the case of AI, the foundation consists of policies, processes, and technology infrastructure.

- Policies provide the rules that govern the adoption, use, and monitoring of AI applications.
- Processes detail how AI use cases are identified, how specific algorithms are developed, and how they are used.
- The technology portion of the foundation ensures the information technology infrastructure needed to support AI is in place.

This chapter provides guidance on building the AI foundation for your organization.

AI Policy Foundation

The starting point for utilizing AI is establishing a set of policies to guide its use. The policies should address the following:

- Guiding principles;
- Governance framework;
- Legal and regulatory compliance;
- Procurement policies;
- Ethics;
- Monitoring, evaluation, and improvement;
- Incident management.

What are some of the key elements or areas that should be included in an AI policy document?

We explore each aspect of the AI foundation below.

Guiding Principles

These policies provide the overall direction for adopting AI. Think of them as the guardrails that ensure the use of AI is consistent with the norms and values of the community. The principles begin with the ethical and equitable use of AI. Fairness, accountability, and accessibility are embedded in all AI use. There is also a commitment to transparency in the decision-making associated with identifying use cases, developing and using algorithms, and monitoring outcomes. The public has a right to know and should not have to work hard to find the information. Another principle is human-in-the-loop. AI facilitates human work, but there is still a human watching the AI decisions and impacts whose responsibility is to make midcourse corrections to keep the AI in line with the original vision of its role.

The foregoing principles are common to all organizations. Your organization might need additional guardrails. Governments concerned about job displacement might look at making investments in retraining to ensure their employees' skills meet the workforce demands of the future, or follow New York State's law on AI that prohibits cutting work hours or replacing personnel because of AI.[1]

The guidelines used by the state of Massachusetts provide a helpful example. In their "Enterprise Use and Development of Generative Artificial Intelligence Policy,"[2] the Commonwealth, while recognizing the advantages AI can bring, establishes certain guidelines for its application within its departments, related to:

- Validation and reliability (there must be regular and high-quality validation processes and checks in place to ensure AI is producing good output);

- Safety, security, and resiliency (any AI used in the Commonwealth should be designed with a high level of safety and security features built in);

- Accountability (AI users should be held accountable for the performance and impact of the AI content they generate and use);

- System and procedural transparency (agencies should keep records regarding the testing, datasets, and modeling in the use of AI);

- Explainability and interpretability (agents should know how AI is making its decisions and recommendations);

- Privacy (AI tools should operate with robust privacy features in place);

- Fairness with mitigation of harmful bias (AI should be used in such a way as to respect, serve, and protect humans' personal and cultural sense of identity, and physical and mental integrity, and agents should regularly evaluate their AI tools for bias or discrimination);

- Know your content (all content made by AI should be properly labeled, and users should be able to know what data AI used to create that content).

The goal of investing time in developing these principles and securing buy-in for them is establishing trust between your organization and the public. AI is a scary unknown for many people. Fears range from job loss to the spread of misinformation to excessive government surveillance. Guiding principles like these help to reduce anxiety.

Governance Framework

The right governance structure is needed to ensure the guiding principles are adopted and if they are not, corrective actions take place. Roles and responsibilities of government employees, staff, and leadership, must be unambiguous. The same is true for external providers. The decision-making and approval process must be documented. What are the process steps to identifying use cases, establishing priorities, sourcing and implementing the technology, and monitoring outcomes?

Good governance requires strong oversight. An AI oversight committee is a helpful structure. The committee should include staff and leadership representatives from your organizations. Avoid people who have direct authority for AI; you don't want the fox guarding the henhouse. You might also include outsiders: some constituents, AI ethics-focused academics, and AI practitioners provide balanced perspectives.

In New York City, for example, the Chief Technology Officer has set up an AI Steering Committee composed of twenty-three representatives from sixteen city agencies, and a broader AI Advisory Network, which includes subject matter experts from the private sector and academia—both of which will advance core initiatives around "designing and implementing a robust governance framework and building external partnerships," guiding principles, and recommendations on the uses and risks of generative AI tools.[3]

> If your government or department establishes an AI steering committee, who should be a part of it (be specific!)?
> ____
> ____
> ____

Even as you are creating your committees and using them to develop broader strategies, it is reasonable to put in place some basic interim guiding principles to give your teams a place to start as they explore AI. While it is building a broader strategy, for instance, San Jose has implemented the following seven key guidelines:

1. Information you enter into Generative AI systems could be subject to a Public Records Act (PRA) request. (. . .) Do not submit any information to a Generative AI platform that should not be available to the general public (such as confidential or personally identifiable information).

2. Review, revise, and fact-check via multiple sources any output from a Generative AI. Users are responsible for any material created with AI support.

3. Cite and record your usage of Generative AI.

4. Create an account just for City use to ensure public records are kept separate from personal records. If a user agrees to the terms and conditions of a system that the City does not have a formal agreement with, he/she is responsible for complying with those terms and conditions.

5. Departments may provide additional rules around Generative AI. Consult your manager or department contact if there are additional department-specific rules.

6. Refer to this document quarterly, as guidance will change with the technology, laws, and industry best practices.

7. Users are encouraged to participate in the City's established workgroups to help advance AI usage best practices in the City and enhance the guidelines.[4]

Legal and Regulatory Compliance

The AI development must be clearly within the bounds of the relevant laws and regulations. Data privacy and data security are the starting point. Most governments have rules about data privacy. Canada's Privacy Act provides an example. The Act stipulates that governments can only use your personal information for the specific reason it was collected, and any use beyond that requires additional consent. Disclosure may be permitted in certain situations like complying with a court order or in federal proceedings, but users always have the right to access their personal information held by government institutions and can request corrections if needed. The Act also outlines how users can make complaints regarding inappropriate use of their data. Data security is complementary. Data breaches at the federal, state, and municipal level highlight the need for vigilance. This is especially true for AI applications, as they often bring together a number of different databases. The more databases, the greater the risk.

Do you know which laws at the federal, state, or local level would govern or impact your ability to use AI tools within your organization?

____

____

____

____

Increasingly, there are AI-specific regulations. At the federal level, for example, the Biden Administration signed multiple policies related to AI vis-à-vis data privacy and security. The "Executive Order on Safe, Security, and Trustworthy Development and Use of AI" (2023)[5] directed federal agencies to develop guidelines for AI systems that handle personal data, ensuring they align with privacy laws, and specifically focused on protecting biometric data such as facial recognition and voiceprint from misuse. It also encouraged AI watermarking to detect AI-generated content and prevent the spread of deepfakes that could misuse personal data. (Note that President Trump rescinded this Executive Order in January 2025.)

The National Security Memorandum on Artificial Intelligence (October 2024)[6] strengthened safeguards for handling personal data and sensitive data in AI-driven security and defense applications and required encryption and security standards for AI models used by government agencies to prevent unauthorized data access. Finally, the "Executive Order to Accelerate AI Infrastructure Development" (2025)[7] directed AI data centers handling personal data to meet federal privacy and cybersecurity standards.

The Trump Administration has signaled its focus regarding AI will be on promoting its development in the United States. This is why he rescinded the 2023 Executive Order, as his administration and its allies viewed the order as being too much of a hindrance on development, such as a requirement that companies building the most powerful AI models share details with the government about those systems before releasing them to the public.[8] Additionally, while the Biden Administration ordered US federal agencies to show their AI tools are not harming the public in order to curb government use of tools that have been found to unfairly discriminate based on race, gender, or disability, the new Order removes those guardrails and explicitly champions developing AI systems "free from ideological bias or engineered social agendas."[9] Until Congress passes AI legislation, there are likely to be policy swings and uncertainty. The implication is to be conservative.

In the absence of federal legislation, states are filling the gap. Colorado's AI Act requires developers and deployers of high-risk AI systems to exercise reasonable care to prevent algorithmic discrimination. It also mandates clear disclosures to consumers regarding the use of AI in decision-making processes.[10] Tennessee's Ensuring Likeness, Voice, and Image Security (ELVIS) Act targets AI-generated deepfakes by prohibiting individuals from using AI to replicate a person's voice or likeness without permission, aiming to protect individuals from unauthorized digital impersonation.[11] There are also municipalities that have codified AI rules. Many have thus far focused on the use of AI in surveillance and decision-making processes, such as facial recognition bans in San Francisco, Portland (OR), and Somerville (MA), but New York City passed a 2021 law (effective January 2023) that mandates that employers conducting business in New York City who use automated employment decision tools must subject these tools to annual bias audits, and are also required to notify candidates about the use of such tools in the hiring process.[12]

Compliance requires verification and, if violations exist, eliminating them. This requires a process. The New York City law noted above offers guidance:

- It outlines the expectations that stakeholders must follow, and how—in this case, stipulating that any employer must subject their AI decision tools to a third-party bias audit no later than one year prior to the date of its use, and that the summary of the results be published on the employer's website prior to the use of the tool. Moreover, the employer must notify each candidate for the job that they are using this tool and disclose the job qualifications that the tool will use in its assessment.

- Given the data-driven nature of AI, it provides additional details on data collection and use—what datasets they are using, where they are acquiring this data, and their data retention and security policy.

- It notes where other legislation may supersede the requirements of this law—that these requirements are void in cases where they would otherwise violate a state or federal law; other regulatory documents also note that in cases where regulations from two levels of government are at odds, the more stringent rule applies.

- It outlines the penalties and parameters of not following the law—$500 for the first violation, and not less than $500 and no more than $1,500 for additional violations, with each day counting as a separate violation and each person who is not informed when the tool is used counting as a separate violation.

- Finally, it details enforcement—the New York City Law Department and its designees may take legal action against anyone failing to comply with the regulations.

Procurement Policies

Every governmental organization has procurement rules. AI contracting must follow these rules. There are, however, nuances that might require additional requirements. Ethics requirements and antibias features might be needed. There are also issues of data protection, use, and ownership. Plans for algorithm updating and retesting also require specification.

> How do you think AI procurement policies might differ from any existing policies your organization has in place? How might they be similar?

There are also issues of using open-source versus proprietary applications. Open-source applications allow for greater flexibility, and if your agency possesses the necessary expertise, your team can adapt the code to meet your specific project requirements. Moreover, code transparency allows for a thorough examination that can help you understand how the tool is working, how it makes its decisions, and generates content. Open-source products can be free, but there may be expenses related to support, maintenance, and the need for outside specialized expertise should you not possess in-house technical knowledge. As well, proprietary software often comes with strong security measures, and its corporate structure can lead to more consistent, controlled development.

The State of California has established procurement policy guidelines, the "State of California GenAI Guidelines for Public Sector Procurement, Uses and

Training,"[13] that can serve as a starting point for you. The document stipulates that the onus is on contracting teams to be aware of AI throughout the procurement process. That is, even when they are not intending to purchase an AI product, they may receive bids that include AI—in areas such as content generation, chatbots, and data analysis, for instance—so when these bids come in, assessing agencies will need to use state AI guidelines and consider impacts of selecting these bids on "security, privacy, workforce, and equity outcomes."[14] In fact, the governance document advises each executive team to designate one person to engage in continuous AI monitoring and review annual employee training to ensure staff understand acceptable use of AI tools.

When seeking AI procurements, an agency must identify the business need and understand the implications of using AI to solve the challenge even before putting anything to tender, which requires a comprehensive discovery process. During this phase, leaders should also create a culture of engagement and open communication with end users to ensure a collaborative and collective approach on the impact of AI technology. The guideline document also provides direction on the risk assessment process to determine the impact of using AI. The state government intends to expand these in the future, including the incorporation of impact on vulnerable communities. Finally, procurement must include a robust testing and feedback framework, not only for the initial purchase phase, but one that will be ongoing throughout the life cycle of the product's use.[15]

Ethics Policies

The foundational policies for AI must include a section on ethics. As with procurement, every government agency has ethics rules. The AI-specific aspects address bias and discrimination, human oversight, and transparency. Policies must be in place that avoid bias and discrimination in the design and use of AI systems. Typical policies include requirements that AI applications be free from bias: government users should know what data their tools used to learn, and how they are applying that data to make decisions; and they should have a process in place to be regularly (annually) testing their platforms to confirm they remain free of bias.

Another dimension of AI ethics involves how humans and AIs interact. What initial and ongoing human intervention is there in the development and ongoing use of AI algorithms? Interaction policies depend on the type of tool used, but if it is public-facing like a chatbot, the public should know when they are engaging with AI rather than with a human. As well, for certain critical processes (and it is up to you to determine what would be considered critical), there needs to be a human in the loop, and any decisions that trigger adverse outcomes for individuals require secondary human review.

Also in the ethics realm are policies regarding transparency. Define the requirements for ensuring stakeholders understand how an AI system is built, its outputs and how the results are used. Besides ensuring that stakeholders know when they are using AI or knowing that AI was involved in an outcome that affected them, departments that use AI should have a dedicated AI ombudsman or steering committee and third-party oversight, with reports made publicly available. Appendix A provides an example of an AI Ethics Policy[16] for an agency to use.

Monitoring, Evaluating, and Improving

Think about the last large systems implementation your organization completed. There was likely a lot of effort put into design to make sure it would have the right functionality and fit. Moreover, energy was expended to ensure its implementation was successful. Once it was up and running, little additional attention was required. This is not the case for AI. Most AI systems are learning and changing as soon as they are put in place. Thus, there is a need to monitor the AI on a continuous basis, evaluate the outputs, and refine the system to improve it with human intervention. If all goes well, the assessment is a light lift. But if not, humans need to intervene with midcourse corrections. The faster issues are identified, the easier it will be to resolve them.

The following principles, pulling together policies from the White House Executive Order on Promoting the Use of Trustworthy AI in the Federal Government, the General Services Administration's AI compliance plan, and the Department of Homeland Security's responsible AI Use document, provide a good starting point for you to customize one of your own.

Continuous Monitoring

- Implement ongoing monitoring mechanisms to assess AI system performance, accuracy, and compliance with ethical guidelines.

- Regularly review AI outputs to identify and mitigate biases, errors, or unintended consequences.

Evaluation and Reporting

- Conduct periodic evaluations of AI systems to determine their impact, effectiveness, and alignment with organizational objectives.

- Document evaluation findings and report them to relevant stakeholders, including oversight bodies and the public, as appropriate.

Risk Management

- Identify potential risks associated with AI systems, including ethical, legal, and operational risks.

- Develop and implement mitigation strategies to address identified risks proactively.

Transparency and Accountability

- Maintain clear documentation of AI system design, data sources, decision-making processes, and evaluation outcomes.

- Ensure accountability by assigning responsibilities for monitoring and evaluation activities to designated personnel or committees.

Stakeholder Engagement

- Engage with internal and external stakeholders, including the public, to gather feedback on AI system performance and societal impacts.

- Incorporate stakeholder input into the continuous improvement of AI systems and related policies.

Implementation

- Develop standard operating procedures (SOPs) for the monitoring and evaluation of AI systems.

- Provide training to relevant personnel on monitoring tools, evaluation methodologies, and ethical considerations.

- Allocate resources to support effective monitoring and evaluation activities.

Incident Management

Incident management policies begin with a definition of an incident and a classification based on severity. Elements might include a data breach, evidence of bias, inaccurate information, or user/public complaints. Next, a pathway for reporting incidents is required. It might be an online form, a hotline, or integrated into an existing reporting mechanism such as 311.

The response protocol defines the steps to investigate and, if needed remediate the problem and the associated roles and responsibilities. These typically include:

- Step 1: Document the issue—nature, size/scale, evidence of failure.
- Step 2: Conduct root cause analysis—get to the sources of the problem.
- Step 3: Define remediation actions—process, policy, people, technology.
- Step 4: Fulfill any legal/compliance requirements—reporting, documentation, communications.
- Step 5: Provide feedback—close the loop with the person/people who raised the issue.

A communications plan is also part of the incident policy. Trust is essential for successful AI. Anything that undermines trust must be addressed. The only thing worse than a failure is one that is unreported, or worse yet, hidden. Transparency is paramount.

While governments at all levels are still in the development stage of crafting AI-specific incident management plans, conventional incident management plans related to cybersecurity and privacy more broadly can provide a useful starting point for those looking to build AI plans. The US Cybersecurity & Infrastructure Security Agency has robust "Cybersecurity Incident & Vulnerability Response Playbooks"[17] with sections on the response process, detection, containment, eradication, post-incident activities, and coordination, along with a useful Incident Response Checklist. The 2017 federal Office of Management and Budget's "Preparing for and Responding to a Breach of Personally Identifiable Information"[18] offers a generalized overview of the key elements of an incident management plan, and the Department of Homeland

Security's "Privacy Incident Handling Guidance"[19] provides a specific example of many of the key elements in place that we noted above.

> Are you familiar with your current incident management plans and policies; if so, what elements do you think can be repurposed for AI applications?
> ____
> ____
> ____
> ____

AI Process Foundation

A strong process for identifying, prioritizing, and implementing AI complements the policies detailed above. In Chapter 9, we outline this identification-implementation process in detail. It begins with stakeholders recognizing that the goal is to identify and fix pain points, rather than just implementing AI for AI's sake; AI has to be the best solution, not just a solution, if you are going to pursue it. Given the power of this technology, the best approach is to go slow, taking on manageable pilots with robust assessment and feedback processes. As part of a pilot approach, you will want to rent rather than buy to develop understanding and experience and develop a system to understand and control risks.

Throughout this process, it is important to engage leadership and those whose jobs are impacted to break down barriers and reluctance right from the outset—change is coming, and you want to reduce the fear of the unknown as it comes. Begin the process by profiling core functions to identify critical tasks and assess their importance and performance. This involves mapping stakeholder expectations, assessing their power and interest, and determining which functions are most vital while considering AI's margin of error. Next, you need to prioritize any critical functions with substantial performance gaps based on quantitative and qualitative measures. This step also considers user segmentation, geographic differences, and equity concerns to refine priorities.

The third step involves identifying AI applications that address high-priority "reds," distinguishing between AI-appropriate and non-AI solutions. It emphasizes leveraging existing AI applications from public sector inventories, private sector innovations, and AI provider solutions while assessing data availability and risk mitigation strategies. The fourth step assesses AI solutions through a benefit-cost analysis, considering financial impact, accuracy improvements, customer time savings, ancillary benefits, and reputational gains. It also evaluates risks, including operational, reputational, and capacity constraints, while weighing build-vs-buy decisions. The fifth step prioritizes AI solutions, aligning them with the organization's strategy and developing a roadmap for implementation. The sixth and final step involves piloting AI applications in low-risk environments to test their viability before full-scale deployment. Here, you want to underpromise and overdeliver, so as not to overinflate expectations and lead to difficulty down the road if stakeholders are disappointed with the first trial.

Implementing policies like the ones we have outlined above is a key to success when it comes to AI. Because these systems are so dense, however, beyond policy you need to also ensure your agency has the technological capacity and know-how to accommodate AI's significant requirements, which we outline in Chapter 6.

Write the key insights you take from the chapter and how it is relevant to bringing AI into your organization.

Chapter 6

AI Technology Foundation

Chapter Summary

From a technical perspective, AI requires robust data infrastructure, computing power, and security. Scalable data storage solutions, encryption, and privacy policies protect sensitive information, while cybersecurity measures and backup strategies ensure operational continuity. Ultimately, responsible AI deployment hinges on thoughtful policy development, careful implementation, and ongoing oversight. By balancing technological advancement with ethical considerations, organizations can harness AI's power while maintaining public trust.

Learning Questions and Food for Thought

1. Data privacy is key when using AI. Who within your own organization can help guide you on how to ensure data privacy in the implementation and use of AI?
2. Are you familiar with existing policies within your organization around cybersecurity?

AI is technology heavy. You need the computer programming that delivers the end service like a chatbot or resume screener. But you also need:

- Data infrastructure;
- Computing power;
- AI tools and platforms;
- Cybersecurity and operations continuity.

As you read the technology requirements, remember: crawl, walk, run. You do not need all the capabilities on Day 1. Focus on what is required for your first pilot, then another, and then a more comprehensive technology suite. Also, many of the needs and expertise to use them can be provided by third parties. Some of the needs will simply require a bolt-on to existing technology. Others will necessitate adding new capabilities.

When it comes to technology infrastructure, your IT team is your best friend!

Data Infrastructure

Data infrastructure addresses how information will be gathered and stored. AI is data intensive and therefore you need the capacity to store and retrieve large datasets that come from various departments and systems. Scalable data storage is accomplished via data lakes or data warehouses. Data lakes typically store raw data while data warehouses maintain clean data for specific applications. Data lakes are offered by Amazon S3 and Azure. Snowflake and Google BigQuery provide data warehouses.

Having the data is necessary but not sufficient. You need the ability to clean, load, and use the information. Cleaning includes identifying and resolving missing or inaccurate data. There are automated tools to do so, including Python, Spark, and AWS Glue. Transformation takes the raw data and formats it for use in AI applications. Extract, transform, load (ETL) pipelines such as Airflow and Apache Beam facilitate this process. For sensitive data, anonymization is required. A general rule of thumb is to anonymize any data in the public domain. There is, however, a trade-off between the level of protection from anonymization and the utility of the data. There are a range of options. Synthetic data generation, homomorphic encryption, and secure multiparty computation are effective platforms.[1] The names sound intimidating; the right solution is to find the expert in your organization on data privacy who can guide your decision process.

Data governance accompanies the digital infrastructure. Here, you need protocols for cataloging the data, controlling access to the data, and monitoring compliance with privacy laws. In 2018, the US Congress enacted The Foundations for Evidence-Based Policymaking Act[2] that has very specific requirements for data governance at the federal level, and depending on your level and the complexity of using AI within your organization, these extensive guidelines—including provisions on setting up a Data Governance Steering Committee—may become useful. However, as Josh Sandler, cofounder of Truetax, a generative AI platform that helps governments provide a better tax-filing experience, argues, for most government agencies, especially in the "crawl" stage, it is not necessary to overly complicate their processes.

To that end, the Federal Trade Commission (FTC) has developed a guide[3] for businesses, written in plain language, that provides the foundation for a data governance plan (intended for private companies, but relevant to public agencies as well). They note there are five principles for data management:

- Know what information you have in your files and on your computers.

- Keep only what you need.

- Protect the information that you keep.

- Properly dispose of what you no longer need.

- Create a plan to respond to security incidents.

<table>
<tr><td>Data privacy is key when using AI. Who within your own organization can help guide you on how to ensure data privacy in the implementation and use of AI?

____
____
____
__________________________________</td></tr>
</table>

You need to ensure you are following privacy law. As of 2025, there is no comprehensive federal policy on privacy, but many states do have their own regulations, which you would need to adhere to depending on your location. The International Association of Privacy Professionals (IAPP) maintains a US State Privacy Legislation Tracker,[4] so if you are not familiar with your existing state policy, you can use this tool to view your local laws.

While the above FTC guidelines are all useful, we will focus on items two and three for the moment. When gathering data for your AI projects, be thoughtful about what you need, and limit yourself to keeping only that information, and only for as long as it is needed. Ensure it is properly labeled and consult with your IT professionals on using metadata to properly label the information you store.

Managing the information you keep is based on four pillars: physical security, electronic security, employee training, and the security practices of your contractors and service providers, the latter three being the most relevant for AI data management. You will want to work with your IT security team to ensure you have standard security protocols in place, such as end-to-end encryption and data isolation, but then provide strong training to your team, as an error on their part when managing sensitive data can result in a vulnerability. Finally, outline expectations with any third-party operators when sharing data with them; Appendix B offers a sample.

Computing Power

AI is a computing power hog. The combination of CPUs, storage, and electricity can become a significant expense. Depending on the application, different resources are needed. Tapping into generative AI with LLMs minimizes your organization's investment in computing power. You leverage the resources of OpenAI, Anthropic, Microsoft, Google, and others. The downsides of this approach are threefold. First, LLMs have limited capabilities. They are great for writing job descriptions or summarizing meeting notes, but they may not have up-to-date knowledge of a given topic (unless they are connected to live data sources), and they may generate inaccurate or hallucinated information. Second, it is harder to secure your data. Unless you have an agreement with the LLM, sometimes what you upload to their platform becomes part of their content; however, a growing number of platforms (including Microsoft Co-Pilot and ChatGPT) now allow you to delete your data and others (like OpenAI) even permit you to opt out of being used for training their system. Third, these applications are free today but may not be in the future. The LLM providers are significantly subsidizing the use of their tools. Sooner or later, they will need to recoup their investment.

If you are developing customized algorithms, you will incur the cost of providing the computing power. The capacity can be rented through entities such as AWS, Google Cloud Storage, or IBM Cloud Storage. When assessing your data needs, key factors to consider are:

- Security: ensure the provider offers strong encryption and complies with relevant data protection regulations.[5]

- Performance: evaluate data transfer speeds and the provider's network infrastructure to ensure it meets your application's performance requirements.[6]

- Pricing: compare storage costs, data retrieval fees, and any additional charges to find a solution that fits your budget.[7]

- Scalability: choose a provider that can accommodate your data growth without compromising performance.[8]

- Reliability: look into the provider's uptime guarantees and historical performance to ensure data availability.[9]

- Integration: consider how well the storage service integrates with your existing tools and workflows.

AI Development Tools and Platforms

A range of AI-specific tools and platforms support the development and use of AI programs. Integrated development environments (IDEs) provide a place to code, debug, and visualize AI applications. Examples of these tools are Jupyter Notebooks, PyCharm, and Visual Studio Code. The US National Institutes of Health, for example, built its NIH Cloud Lab that offers researchers a number of AI-driven tools to facilitate data analysis. They developed much of the platform using Jupyter Notebooks, an open-source web-based application for data analysis and machine learning development that enables users to conduct AI-assisted data analysis involving large datasets and extensive computations.[10]

There are a number of frameworks that provide building blocks for machine learning and deep learning. Frameworks like TensorFlow, PyTorch, and Keras help developers and researchers easily create and optimize neural networks for various tasks like image recognition and natural language processing. All are designed for different use cases, with Keras being the simplest and designed for those new to deep learning platforms, and PyTorch and TensorFlow better suited to more advanced, larger-scale project developers.

Successful AI applications are predicated on great data. Unfortunately, data is rarely great when you get it. There are tools to clean and prepare the data for use. OpenRefine and DataRobot Paxata combine, clean, and transform datasets. Labelbox is an example of a tool for annotating images, text, and video for use in training algorithms.

Large Language Models (LLMs) are also tools, a type of AI that processes and generates human-like text using vast amounts of training data. These models are based on deep learning, specifically transformer architectures (like GPT, BERT, LLaMA). They excel at understanding, generating, and analyzing natural language. Trained on massive datasets (of books, articles, scientific papers, government records, etc.), they use billions (or even trillions) of parameters to make predictions and can perform tasks like summarization, translation, chatbots, sentiment analysis, and document processing.

The US Department of Veterans Affairs is leveraging LLMs like Med-PaLM 2 to analyze patient records, summarize medical histories, and flag high-risk individuals for better healthcare prioritization, ultimately improving efficiency and patient outcomes.[11] Similarly, the National Institutes of Health is utilizing BioBERT and other AI models to process vast volumes of medical research, enabling faster literature reviews and accelerating biomedical discoveries for diseases like cancer and Alzheimer's.[12] Meanwhile, the Department of Defense employs GPT-based models in its Project Maven to automate intelligence analysis, extracting key insights from surveillance data and foreign language reports, enhancing decision-making and threat detection capabilities for national security.[13]

A final toolkit provides a visualization of model outputs. Tableau and Power BI are popular examples of business intelligence tools used for data visualization, analysis, and reporting. They help organizations turn raw data into interactive dashboards, graphs, and insights for decision-making. Multiple federal departments use these tools, such as the Centers for Disease Control to track and visualize disease outbreaks in real time, and the Department of Veterans Affairs to analyze healthcare data, aiming to improve patient outcomes and operational efficiency.[14] Many governments at all levels used Tableau to develop dashboards showing Covid cases during the Covid pandemic, including the state of Ohio, Dallas (TX), and Lake County (IL).[15]

Cybersecurity and Operations Continuity

AI application adoption requires concurrent AI cybersecurity. Data encryption, access control, and incident response tools are required. The Federal Trade Commission's guide[16] offers a great starting point for ensuring you have all the key elements of a policy covered.

Operations continuity applies to all systems including AI. Specific AI backup infrastructure is needed to ensure continuity of operations, especially if your AI application is operating in real time and directly impacts constituent services. A starting point is backup data. Depending on the application, you can use real-time or periodic backup. Real-time backup is just that; it provides continual refresh of the information in a secure locale. This is most appropriate for mission-critical datasets where loss would be unacceptable, such as in high-risk or highly regulated areas like defense and finance. Periodic or incremental backup is more cost-effective and would work for applications with less critical applications and/or those with stable datasets that do not have online connectivity, and AI tools focused on development or historical records that are not changing frequently. Distributing the backup infrastructure across geography is a way to reduce the risk of region-specific issues such as earthquakes, hurricanes, and wildfires.

> Are you familiar with existing policies within your organization around cybersecurity?
>
> ____
> ____
> ____
> ____

The AI models themselves require backup. Maintaining all versions of models not only provides protection in the case of corruption, malware, etc., but also offers a source to trace back changes if bugs are found. In some cases, local versions of global applications can be maintained in case the central platform is down.

A last consideration regarding backup is ensuring your vendors have a continuity plan and that you will be protected. Language can be added to the contract for your protection. The public is not interested in hearing that the failure is a result of a vendor issue; they expect you to prevent the problem. In Appendix C, we provide some sample language that offers the key elements that government agencies may want to include in their contracts with AI systems providers. From here, we look at how you can begin pulling together the expertise necessary for AI adoption.

> Write the key insights you take from the chapter and how it is relevant to bringing AI into your organization.
>
> ____
> ____
> ____
> ____

Chapter 7

Developing Necessary Expertise and Infrastructure

Chapter Summary

Successful AI adoption requires a combination of traditional and AI-specific skills. Applying AI to improve service delivery and decision-making is similar to more traditional improvement efforts from process reengineering to adopting new computer systems. AI also requires technical skills, including an understanding of machine learning, data science, systems integration, and cybersecurity. AI adoption also requires an understanding of regulations at the municipal, state, and federal levels. Comfort with making ethical decisions is an additional requirement. A final requirement is comfort operating under uncertainty. Here, the key is being able to quickly absorb information, chart a path, and execute it. An organizational expertise assessment will identify the strengths and gaps of your team.

The options for filling gaps include an AI training program, learning from the AI community, hiring consultants, and hiring staff. The primary goal of the training is to ensure those impacted directly or indirectly by using AI have a basic understanding of the what and why of AI. Secondary goals are to provide technical training for those directly involved in the identification and implementation of use cases, enable leadership to set the right AI guiding policies, and leverage the power of AI throughout the organization. Learning from the AI community includes AI providers, academics, and other government agencies. The Government AI Coalition hosted by San Jose is a great starting point. Consultants can provide specific expertise at a known cost, but it can be expensive, and there is a risk of becoming dependent. The final option is hiring staff, which is great for building long-term expertise, but these people are in high demand and may come with a steep price tag.

> ## Learning Questions and Food for Thought
>
> 1. How well positioned is your organization to complete improvement projects?
> 2. What is your assessment of your group's AI capabilities?
> 3. What would you include in an AI training program for your organization?
> 4. How might you tap the AI community to build your AI capacity?

Rio de Janeiro is famous for its stunning natural landscape, loud Carnival festivities, incredible nightlife, and hip-gyrating Latin music. But as recently as a few years ago, if you were to walk through many of its neighborhoods, your nostrils might be hit not by the smells wafting from Brazilian steakhouses but the scent of rotting garbage, and your eyes would be more likely to be drawn to looking at the bags of refuse spilling out onto the road than colorful Carnival costumes.

The problem was that refuse collection had gotten out of control of the local government, with some incredibly damaging impacts. While the impact was felt across the sprawling city, a major symbol was the fetid waters of Guanabara Bay. Once a sparkling blue oasis teeming with sea life including playful dolphins, today this UNESCO World Heritage Site is one of the most polluted coastal ecosystems in the world, filled with domestic garbage, industrial waste, even corpses.[1]

Thankfully for local citizens and conservationists the world over, in the last few years the national government has worked with local authorities to come up with solutions to widespread mismanagement of waste. There were many challenges, but a big issue was that inefficient collection routes left bins unemptied for far too long, often forcing citizens to take matters into their own hands. Moreover, costs were astronomical, and many items that could easily be recycled were ending up in landfills due to poor planning.

Looking at the challenge holistically, stakeholders recognized that what they faced was an analytics problem—how could they pick up trash more efficiently, but not so often that it led to additional costs? After analyzing a number of different solution sets, they settled on adopting AI and Internet of Things capabilities throughout their waste management system. They added sensors to garbage bins that would alert the system when the bin was full, so a truck would only stop to collect waste when it was necessary.[2] To facilitate more recycling, officials installed AI optical separators, capable of classifying film, paper, cardboard, and other waste based on characteristics like chemical composition, shape, and color.[3]

Most successfully of all, they started using an AI tool to analyze past demand to forecast where waste would be in the future, and had the software create waste collection routes. Thanks to these new routes, Rio became one of only a handful of Latin American cities to have a 100 percent collection rate coverage, and it was able to cut collection costs by 45 percent.[4]

This Rio success story is impressive, but it did not happen by accident. It came about through a process of identifying root causes, looking at the range of possible solutions available, and selecting a comprehensive solution set that addressed the dynamic needs of a city struggling to get garbage off its streets. For most organizations, adopting AI will similarly require building technical, regulatory, and operational capacity. This chapter highlights the requirements, provides a self-assessment of your specific needs, and offers guidance on how to fill the gaps.

Technical Expertise

Successful AI adoption requires a combination of traditional and AI-specific skills. Applying AI to improve service delivery and decision-making is similar to more traditional improvement efforts from process reengineering to adopting new computer systems. Adopting any improvement initiative, including AI, follows a similar pattern. The starting point is defining the problem. As Albert Einstein was supposed to have said: "If I had an hour to solve a problem, I'd spend fifty-five minutes thinking about the problem and five minutes thinking about solution."[5] While this is hyperbole, it does highlight the need to make sure you are solving the correct problem.

Next comes gathering evidence to understand the impacts of the problem and its root causes. Here stakeholder analysis reveals not only who is impacted and to what degree but also what the interests and motivations are of those who are needed to solve the issue. Understanding the root causes directs the focus on solutions. Avoid addressing the proximate or surface causes without also resolving the root issues. If you have dandelions in your lawn, you can cut off the bloom, but the flower will return in days. Pull out the root and you permanently solve the problem.

Finding problem fixes, solutionizing, is the exciting stage. We have a number of tools to facilitate identifying short- and long-term solutions.

Wherever possible, run a pilot to test the solutions and make sure that theory translates into success in the real world. Mark teaches a case about a rehabilitation hospital that shifted its approach from a generalist model to a specialist model. The problem to be solved was making sure the patient received the best care possible and discharging them as quickly as possible. A physical therapist today works with stroke, cardiac, and pulmonary patients. In the future, the therapist whose specialty is with stroke patients only works with stroke patients. The program was implemented without a pilot and was disastrous. The utilization of the therapist plummeted, and faster discharge led to less hospital income. The moral of the story: always test your ideas in a controlled environment before going all in. Learning from the pilot, the program is refined and taken to scale.

The technical expertise to manage improvement projects includes:

- Strategic thinking: understanding the impact of the problem on the organization and how alternative solutions align with its strategic direction. Considering the risk profile of the problem and solution.

- Managerial skills: building a project team, making a project plan, directing the execution of the plan, helping overcome barriers.

- Interpersonal skills: developing the best team and ensuring they function well internally and externally.

- Engagement abilities: knowing whose involvement is needed as well as recruiting them into the process (and keeping them involved).

- Communication abilities: customizing how and when to share information with stakeholders in ways that reach their heads and hearts.

In addition, there is the need for subject matter expertise. If you are implementing an IT system to identify tax fraud, you need knowledge of the tax code, tax avoidance strategies, fraud detection best practices, and so on. Reengineering the restaurant licensing process requires a team that can map the process, identify the bottleneck, understand current statutes, and propose a new process that is high quality, efficient, and equitable.

Organizations typically have many of these skills; what is additionally required for successful AI adoption? AI-specific requirements center on three areas: AI technical expertise, AI ethics and regulations, and operating under uncertainty. Let's look at each of these in more detail.

> What is your overall assessment of your group's AI capabilities?
>
> ____
>
> ____
>
> ____
>
> ____

AI Technical Expertise

AI technical expertise consists of an alphabet soup of terms such as R, PyTorch, SQL, and more. The skills begin with an understanding of machine learning. The traditional approach is writing a computer program that provides a detailed set of instructions on how to find tax evasion, for example, such as a mismatch between employer-reported income and filer's income. This works if the rules are correct and comprehensive. The problem is the evaders understand the rules and develop workarounds. Machine learning systems are given examples of tax evaders and non-evaders. The system looks at dozens of attributes about the evaders and non-evaders. Based on the examples, the computer program builds a profile of an evader. The system can look at new cases and identify which are likely to be evaders. Humans determine if the system was correct, and that information is now more of an insight that is used to refine the identification of tax cheats.

Computer languages are used to develop the algorithms. You might remember coding in Basic, Cobol, Fortran, or Java. The languages for AI are Python, TensorFlow, and PyTorch. Python is widely used because it is coded in plain English, it has many uses (web design, data analysis, controlling robots), and there are many premade tools, which increase efficiency.

A second aspect of technical expertise is data science and analytics. This may sound intimidating, but it is nothing more than collecting and cleaning data, conducting analysis, and reporting results. While the tasks are clear, the execution is more complex. Access to comprehensive information is essential to avoid biases being built into AI algorithms. For example, if a school board uses incomplete census data to predict future enrollment, it might underestimate student populations in poorly assessed areas, leaving them unprepared to handle demand down the road (such as lacking sufficient schools or classrooms).

A related area of expertise for AI is data engineering. Here the challenge is to maintain and store the vast amount of information required to run AI algorithms. Questions raised are:

(1) What data needs to be stored and for how long?

(2) What level of protection is required?

(3) What infrastructure is needed and who provides it?

Data issues are especially acute in the public sphere because there are often regulations about public data retention and security. The data are often highly sensitive, including health, education, and public safety information. Moreover, stored information must be readily available to respond to Freedom of Information Act requests.

Systems integration and cybersecurity are also necessary. These skills are common in most computer development efforts. But with AI, there is a distinctive need to pull information from multiple systems that often use different formats, such as tabular data (like Excel spreadsheets or JavaScript Object Notation), real-time or web-scraped data, and plain text documents.

All organizations need to protect their data, especially their customer/constituent information. Mark remembers the first time he got a letter warning that his personal data was compromised by a cyberattack and he should check his bank account and his credit scores. He was panicked. Now, Mark seems to get such a letter every month and barely reacts. The risk in the public sector is high and the resources are often not commensurate with that risk. Constituent data are very sensitive, as mentioned above. There is also the political cost of a data breach. The plight of the director of the federal Office of Personnel Management in the Obama administration is illustrative. The director was forced to resign after hackers stole the Social Security numbers and health information of millions of people.

The risk of data hacks is intensified because the bad guys have more resources than government agencies. Cyber ransom attacks on state and local government have increased dramatically in recent years. Malware and ransomware attacks increased by 148 percent and 51 percent respectively between 2022 and 2023.[6] A 2023 cyberattack in Dallas led to a months-long effort to review and clean City servers. Municipal court, water department billing, and emergency responder computers were compromised. Baltimore faced a ransomware attack several years earlier. The attackers demanded about $75,000 in Bitcoins for restoration of the city's servers. Baltimore did not pay. But cost estimates of the resulting interruption were in the millions of dollars.[7] The root causes of these attacks and others are a lack of preparation, expertise, and funding. AI intensifies the attractiveness of attacks by ransom seekers because there are more entry points into government systems, more data are integrated, and the costs of an outage are high.

AI Ethics and Regulations

AI raises numerous ethical considerations, such as ensuring the data used to train AI tools is not in itself biased, which would cause a perpetuation of that bias in AI outcomes, and concerns over whether the content AI tools create is accurate and true (covered in Chapter 4). Addressing these concerns requires a distinctive skill set. A foundational attribute of people who effectively address ethical dilemmas is a commitment to moral principles even at the expense of efficiency and expediency. Another attribute is empathy, proactively seeking to understand the needs of marginalized individuals and communities and advocating on their behalf. Two others are critical thinking—seeing potential impacts in complex environments—and open-mindedness—considering traditional and nontraditional approaches. A final ingredient in the ethical recipe is courage. There are often strong opposing viewpoints on ethical issues. Having the fortitude to decide and then advocate for it under pressure is essential.

There is also a need for substantive expertise in dealing with moral and ethical issues, especially those associated with AI. Familiarity with ethical decision-making frameworks provides a clear path to frame the ethical issues, identify options, make trade-offs, and develop a consensus for moving forward. A complementary skill set is understanding the specific ethical issues associated with AI. Bias, transparency, privacy, and accountability are particularly relevant in the AI context. Predictive policing tools designed to forecast criminal activity, once heralded with much fanfare, have come under fire because they use historical crime data that studies have found bias them towards disproportionately targeting marginalized communities, and the opaque, proprietary nature of their algorithms can make it difficult for the public or even the agencies using these tools to understand or contest how a decision was made.[8]

Command of legal and regulatory requirements surrounding AI at the municipal, state, federal, and international level is a required asset. The AI regulatory landscape is best described as developing. Moreover, there is not a single source of AI regulations. Therefore, the expertise required here is to know (1) what to look for; (2) where to find it; and (3) how to interpret it.

At the municipal level there may be ordinances about the collection, use, and protection of constituents' information. To address AI, some cities are adopting guidelines that align AI practices with public interests. New York City's Artificial Intelligence Action Plan, according to Mayor Adams, "will strike a critical balance in the global AI conversation—one that will empower city agencies to deploy technologies that can improve lives while protecting against those that can do harm."[9] The plan includes developing a governance framework, an external advisory network, AI procurement standards, and an annual report.

Some states have adopted AI legislation to provide guardrails for the use of AI in government and to protect the public as AI spreads in all domains. In 2024, AI-related regulations were proposed in forty-five state legislatures, and thirty-one states adopted resolutions or statutes.[10] The actions cover the spectrum from pronouncing the need for AI policy and creating an AI task force to requiring due care avoiding algorithmic discrimination in high-risk AI systems and making the fraudulent use of deep fakes a crime. More regulations are coming; knowing the rules in your jurisdiction is a requirement for AI deployment.

In the United States, there is not a comprehensive approach to regulating AI at the federal government level. Former president Biden issued an Executive Order in 2023 that seeks to ensure the safe and secure development of AI, with required actions including stress testing AI algorithms, sharing test results with the federal government, watermarking content to identify deepfakes, using privacy protection tools, and encouraging community engagement. However, President Trump rescinded that order within his first few days in office in 2025 and has ordered a review of every policy, directive, and order made as a result of Biden's 2023 executive order to ensure that nothing inhibits AI's development in a manner that promotes "human flourishing, economic competitiveness, and national security."[11] How this new mandate will change the approach of the federal government as it relates to AI over the next four years remains to be seen.

Looking across the globe, we see a patchwork of AI regulations. The European Union has the most comprehensive framework detailed in the EU AI Act. Their approach is to regulate AI based on risk. The higher the risk, the greater the scrutiny. The framework also includes very high-risk AI systems that are prohibited, such as those that manipulate behavior or engage in social scoring. The Act also includes transparency and disclosure requirements for

AI EXPERTISE

A Technical Expertise
- Machine Learning
- Data Science
- Computer Languages
- Data Engineering
- Systems Integration
- Cyber Security

AI Ethics and Regulations
- Legal and Regulatory Requirements
- Ethical Decision-Making Frameworks

Operating Under Uncertainty
- Agile Mindset
- Scenario Planning Frameworks

Figure 7.1 AI expertise. Generated by the authors.

higher risk algorithms. There are also enforcement mechanisms to ensure compliance.

The descriptions above are a snapshot in time. The particular expertise required in your team will be what allows you to keep pace with the evolution of regulations and determine how they impact your AI aspirations. Figure 7.1 summarizes the types of expertise you will likely need.

Operating Under Uncertainty

Turning to the third requirement for successful AI adoption, we need to remember that AI is a work in progress. What the future holds is very difficult to forecast. Therefore, you need people on your team who are skilled in decision-making under uncertainty. The general skills for surviving or hopefully thriving in an uncertain world begin with an agile mindset. This is the ability to quickly absorb information and adjust your thinking and not become overwhelmed by change. Another attribute is forward-looking intuition: this means being able to look around the corner at what is coming with a reasonable degree of accuracy, and looking at information and seeing trends as well as disruptions. A third skill is being able to simultaneously see the big picture and its constituent parts. Scenario planning frameworks can provide a structured approach for moving forward in an uncertain world.[12]

Ben spends part of his life in a very uncertain world. He is a first responder to wildfires in British Columbia, Canada. When his team arrives at a fire site, just as with Albert Einstein, they take the time to both look at digital maps and also ground-truth the scene (i.e., walk around or take a ride in a helicopter) in order to understand what reality looks like on the ground. For example, what

AI SELF-ASSESSMENT

CRITERIA	**ASSESSMENT**
	Weak ———————————————————▶ Strong

Leadership and Strategy

Governance and Policy

Data Readiness

Technology Infrastructure

Workforce and Skills

Budget and Resource Allocation

Risk Management/Monitoring

Ethical and Social Impact

Figure 7.2 AI self-assessment. Generated by the authors.

assets exist that you can use to your advantage—such as bodies of water or rocky outcrops free from flammable materials? In an uncertain fire, you *can* be confident that in most situations the fire will have a hard time jumping over the water or the rocks, so you can focus more on the areas where there is greater uncertainty. Moreover, the firefighters can use these geographic traits to their advantage, anchoring a fire line off a rocky outcrop and pumping water from the stream, for example.

To put this in an AI context, take the time now to understand what your assets are—whether those are the skills of your team, the connections you have with other departments, existing technology or infrastructure, or anything else that might be useful as you grapple with future challenges.

Figure 7.2 provides a framework for the assessment. More details are provided in Appendix D.

Firstly, this will help prioritize your areas of focus—in your rush to adopt AI, you don't throw out older software that might already be performing very well and ignore weaker areas. Secondly, it will help you to think about how you can take those existing strengths and potentially make them more efficient with AI tools where appropriate. Lastly, in a world of uncertainty, some things are more certain than others; there is greater certainty about how a fire near the water's edge will spread than one in areas with more fuel, influenced by wind and sun. What are the areas of greater certainty and uncertainty within your own operations—are there universal truths or elements that will likely stay the same? How will you monitor future changes, and how often? To get started, use the self-assessment questions we have included in Appendix D.

<table>
<tr><td>What is your overall assessment of your group's AI capabilities?

____

____

____

____</td></tr>
</table>

Filling the Gaps

The diagnostic in Appendix D highlights the gaps to be filled. The options for filling the gaps include an AI training program, learning from the AI community, hiring consultants, and hiring staff.

AI Training Program

A starting point is providing the team with a focused AI training program. The program can be developed and delivered leveraging internal expertise. Content and insights from outside experts can plug any holes.

The primary goal of the training is to ensure those impacted directly or indirectly by using AI have a basic understand of why AI is being used. Borrowing from a retailer in Boston that says, "An educated consumer is our best customer," let's state that secondary goals are to provide technical training for those directly involved in the identification and implementation of use cases, enable leadership to set the right AI guiding policies, and leverage the power of AI throughout the organization.

A multiphase training program allows for the right people to be in the room and time to digest the content. Our experience has shown that ninety-minute sessions are optimal. These provide enough time to dive into the content, but they are not so long that people become overwhelmed or distracted. The following is a sample plan for a multiphase training program.

Phase 1: AI Basics

The key elements are:

- Introduction to AI and machine learning (ML): definitions, history, and evolution.

- Data basics: understanding data types, sources, and quality.

- AI in government: case studies and potential use cases.

The content here mirrors what we provided in Chapters 2 and 3 of this book. The goal of this phase is for everyone to have a solid grasp of AI. Success is achieved if the participants can understand the discussion of AI in the general media and be able to explain the basics to their parents and/or children. Moreover, they can see how AI can improve their lives and add value for constituents.

The audience for this phase is broad—leadership, subject matter experts, frontline and back-office staff. The more people who understand AI, the better. In Chapter 8, we explore how to sell the idea of adopting AI to the organization. The more people are educated about AI, the less fear there will be, and the easier it will be to move forward with AI use cases. It will also increase the likelihood of successful implementation.

Phase 2: Policy and Protection

Adopting AI in any organization requires policies and guardrails to make sure the expected value of AI is achieved and that risks are mitigated. The training content here focuses on:

- Strategic Alignment: AI use cases that support organizational goals.
- AI Ethics and Bias Mitigation: fairness, accountability, and transparency.
- Regulatory Frameworks: compliance with laws and data privacy.
- Political Realities: interrelationship between AI adoption and political considerations.

The audience for this session skews toward leadership and management, but again the more people who understand these aspects of AI, the better.

This phase is not only about educating the team but also about developing the policies, processes, and guardrails to support AI deployment. To achieve these dual objectives, the phase can be completed in three sessions. The first is teaching. Case examples and simulations are effective in teaching this content. The second is doing and the third is reflecting and refining. Using structured templates is a way to keep the conversation on target and ensure you complete the deliverables.

Phase 3: Technical Expertise

This training is about building the AI "doing" muscle. The content includes:

- Data Science Tools: Python, R, SQL, and data visualization.

- Machine Learning Basics: supervised and unsupervised learning, and model evaluation.

- AI System Integration: APIs, cloud platforms, and legacy systems.

- Cybersecurity Essentials for AI: protecting data and systems.

The audience for this training is limited to technical and subject matter experts who will be developing and using AI applications.

Many organizations rely on outside expertise to specify the content and do the teaching. Getting your hands dirty is the best way to make sure the understanding can take root. Therefore, the session should include coding models and hackathons.

Phase 4: Applications and Implementation

Perhaps the most exciting phase is learning how to identify and implement use cases. The material covered in this session centers on:

- Use Case Development: identifying and prioritizing projects.

- Prototyping AI Solutions: building MVPs (Minimum Viable Products).

- Performance Measurement: KPIs and impact evaluation.

A broader audience is appropriate here. In developing AI, the specific context is important. Therefore, you might conduct a general session with everyone and then subsequent deep dive sessions by department or application.

Sharing examples of how others have tapped AI opportunities is a powerful way of demonstrating the value of AI and providing proof it can be done. This can be followed by real cases in your organization, the more tangible, the better.

Across all phases, provide easy-to-use resources for reference after the training is complete. Videos are especially effective to refresh participants' minds.

\What would you include in an AI training program for your organization?

Learning from the AI Community

A second approach to filling the gaps is learning from the AI community—providers, academics, and other governmental users. Leveraging internal expertise for the training program is important, but tapping into the AI community can broaden and deepen the learning. A good starting point is learning from AI providers. They are truly the experts. OpenAI (the developer of ChatGPT), Anthropic (offers Claude), and Microsoft (provides Copilot AI) are great sources for insight on the use of large learning models (LLMs). You can also tap niche developers to discuss specific AI applications that are relevant to meet your needs.

Many AI companies look for beta test sites for their products. You provide the site for testing; they contribute the algorithm. It is a win-win. In Boston where Mark lives, Google is providing its AI traffic signal management system, Project Green Light, to reduce traffic congestion in the city by optimizing the signal timing. Another local example is ClearGov, a Massachusetts vendor that introduced an AI-powered tool designed to assist municipalities in crafting budgets and associated narratives. The tool leverages AI to generate contextual explanations for budget figures, facilitating clearer communication with elected officials and citizens. The platform underwent beta testing with various New England governments to refine its functionalities.[13]

Academic institutions are another place for learning. The options here range from reading research papers and attending seminars to building a one-on-one relationship between a university and your organization. How best to tap this resource is determined by the gaps that require filling. An illustrative example is Georgia Tech's AI Hub, which "is dedicated to advancing artificial intelligence research and field deployment through innovation, collaboration, industry partnerships and workforce development."[14] Another example is Stanford's Regulation, Evaluation, and Governance Lab (RegLab), which partners with government agencies to design and evaluate programs, policies, and technologies that modernize government. They are an interdisciplinary team of legal experts, data scientists, social scientists, and engineers who are passionate about building an evidence base and high-impact demonstration projects for improved delivery of government services.

Learning from other government organizations is the third leg of the AI community stool. For a broad perspective, tap into the networks offered by the National Governors Association (NGA) or the US Conference of Mayors (USCOM). The former ran a webinar series looking to mitigate AI risks in state governments, including misinformation and data privacy concerns. They also hosted a session "Navigating the GenAI Frontier: Strategies for Governors' Offices," aimed at helping governors maximize AI benefits while mitigating associated risks in 2024. The USCOM's Mayors Leadership Institute on Smart Cities initiative, in partnership with NYU's Wagner School, helps city leaders leverage AI to enhance urban service delivery. For more specific AI use cases, do some internet, or better yet, LLM research to find near peers with experience.

One especially notable resource is the Government AI Coalition hosted by the city of San Jose, California. The GovAI Coalition is composed of government members from local, state, and federal agencies united in the mission to promote responsible and purposeful AI in the public sector.[15] Their specific objectives are:

1. Using AI for social good;

2. Ensuring ethical, nondiscriminatory, and responsible AI governance;

3. Promoting vendor accountability;

4. Improving government services; and

5. Fostering cross-agency collaboration and knowledge sharing.

They offer a variety of policy and use case resources and templates. The AI Policy Manual template provides a starting point draft covering governance, review, and request for proposal. Another template is for gathering comprehensive information from AI providers. The coalition is open to local, state, and federal government agencies.

Buying Expertise

A third way to fill gaps in expertise is to buy it from consultants. There is no shortage of consultants offering services. A Google search of "AI consultants" returns many sponsored links before the endless stream of others not willing to pay to play. The offerings range includes large and well-known firms as well as less-known boutiques. There are also numerous lists of "Top 10" AI consultants, as well as articles written by consultants touting their work.

The pros of hiring consultants to fill your gaps are knowledge, speed, and minimizing fixed costs. Consultants bring deep expertise in the state of the art as well as the practical use cases that are adding value in other organizations. The consultants have already come down the learning curve on the substance of AI and thus provide a quicker solution than developing the expertise in-house. There is the caveat that the consultants do need some time learning the context and culture of your organization. Consultants are also a variable and known cost. You pay for what you need, no more, so the budget is known. Another caveat: consultants are very good at extending relationships. As a consultant, Mark began thinking about the next project the first day of the initial project. Other advantages of tapping consultants include objectivity, knowledge transfer, and access to the network of the consultant's clients.

The cons center on cost, understanding, and dependency. Consultants charge top dollar for top talent. The cost per hour is often eye-popping. This is a particular challenge in the public sphere where details about consultant arrangements are publicly available. Newspaper reporters love being able to publish headlines like: "Mayor's Office Paying $500 per Hour for AI Consultant." The economic rationale might be strong, but the optics might be deadly. A second concern is how well and quickly the consultant understands your organization's culture and context. It takes time to know who the opinion leaders are, who the subject matter experts are, and who the skeptics are. The latter are notorious for blocking consulting progress. Assuming the consultant is successful, there is a risk of dependence on the consultant. This is mitigated by making sure there is full knowledge transfer during the engagement.

> **What is your assessment of your group's AI capabilities?**
> ____
> ____
> ____
> ____

Answering the following questions can help you determine if engaging a consultant is the right approach.

- What are the gaps and how critical are they?
- What is the cost (financial, time, risk) in closing the gaps internally?
- How applicable is the consulting expertise to our gap?
- What is the time and cost to get the consultant up to speed and add value?
- Will the organization accept the help?
- Is this a one-time need or will it be ongoing support?
- What is the return on investment? (Is the juice worth the squeeze?)

If the gap is critical, the costs for internal solutions are high, the organization will support the consultant, the need is short-term, and the overall return on investment is high, the consulting approach is the way to go.

If you opt for hiring a consultant, here are some suggestions to get the most value from the relationship.

- First and foremost, confirm, confirm, confirm. Clarify the project scope and deliverables, the project manager and the team members, the budget, and timing. Think about what happens if the arrangement is not working out. This is easy to do while you're dating but really hard after the wedding.

- Second, define the working relationship. Who does what with whom in both organizations and how do they collaborate? Who leads the initiative from your side and who else needs to be involved? Establish project processes: meeting frequency, updates, problem resolution, etc.

- Third, address the "data dilemma." What information is needed? What format? When? What are substitutes if data are not accessible? Make sure the consultant has a clear need for the information, enough but not too much. Watch out for broad and/or ambiguous data requests. Chances are the consultant is not sure what is really needed and runs the risk of boiling the ocean in search of answers.

Hiring

The fourth approach to filling the gaps is hiring staff. If you are looking to build long-term AI capabilities, hiring the expertise may be the most effective approach. The decision to hire to meet AI requirements is similar to hiring for any other function. But there are a few important differences. First, AI expertise is in high demand, and the cost of hiring might be prohibitive. This is especially problematic if your organization has defined compensation bands or ranges. Retaining this talent is also difficult. Changing jobs after a short period is very common in the high-tech world.

A second challenge is that the AI use cases are changing rapidly. The need to tap today's opportunities might be very different in a year or two. Also, government priorities change with the ups and downs of the economy and with each new administration. We were working with a city recently on identifying AI use cases and building a roadmap for implementation. When we began the work, the focus was on tapping opportunities to enhance service

FILLING THE GAPS

Approach	Advantages	Limitations
AI TRAINING PROGRAM	• Engage the Full Organization • Customized Focus • Low Cost	• Lack of Inhouse Expertise • Lack of Outside Perspective
LEVERAGING THE AI COMMUNITY	• Tap the Wisdom of Experts • Low Cost • Build Relationships for AI Adoption	• Time Intensive • Need to Provide Context
BUYING EXPERTISE	• Fast and Targeted • Known, Variable Cost • Done and Gone	• Need to Provide Context • Misunderstanding the Culture • High Cost
HIRING EXPERTISE	• Get Exactly What You Need • Build Long-Term Capacity	• Competitive and Costly Market • Locked In if Needs Change

Figure 7.3 Filling the gaps. Generated by the authors.

delivery for constituents. A few months into the effort, the economic winds shifted and we pivoted to AI uses that could help close a budget shortfall.

A third challenge is that the hiring and onboarding process can be lengthy. Four to six months for getting a person on the job is common. Then the new hire needs to find the watercooler and come down the learning curve. If time is of the essence, hiring is not likely the best option.

The Path Forward

Considering the alternatives for filling gaps, we suspect you will need a combination of the actions summarized in Figure 7.3. A common path is:

1. Develop and conduct an AI training program.

2. Conduct an expertise gap analysis.

3. Leverage the AI community to get you smarter.

4. Hire consultants to fill very specific gaps.

5. Pilot some AI applications.

6. Build your AI muscle with more training and very selective hiring.

With an expertise plan in place, it is time to think about how to sell AI to your organization.

> Write the key insights you take from the chapter and how it is relevant to bringing AI into your organization.
> ____
> ____
> ____
> ____

Chapter 8

Selling AI to the Organization

Chapter Summary

Selling the idea of bringing AI into your organization rests upon three principles of change management—change is an unnatural act, change management is a process, and crawl to walk to run. Change is an unknown and therefore rarely comfortable. Think of selling AI as an advocacy campaign. Understand the interests that are threatened and demonstrate that there are significant benefits. Equally important is overcoming inertia by making it easy to say yes. Finally, expect it will take time to build support for AI. Think about the S-shaped adoption curve and who will be your innovators and early adopters. Their success with AI will convince others to join the AI world.

There are multiple frameworks for accomplishing change management. John Kotter's Leading Change model provides a holistic view of the change process—creating a sense of urgency, enlisting a guiding coalition of champions, articulating a strategy, generating quick wins, and institutionalizing the change. Adaptive Leadership zeroes in on how human emotions like fear and loss are barriers to change and how you can minimize these barriers by acknowledging the emotions. Also, involve those impacted by AI initiatives in the design, development and implementation, and evaluation of the system. The Human Element explains that "progressive fuel" (the benefits) is overshadowed by the "aversive fuel" (the concerns). The concerns are (1) inertia—too overwhelming; (2) effort—too much work and an unclear plan; (3) emotion—risk of loss; and (4) reactance—a violation of my beliefs. You can overcome the barriers by starting small and demonstrating that the change is done in bite-sized chunks. A powerful complement is having an internal opinion leader or external change agent attest to the feasibility of the proposed AI system. Provide a clear roadmap, simple steps, and sufficient resources to get the job done right.

Don't forget to use your basic persuasion skills!

Learning Questions and Food for Thought

1. What are the barriers you envision to selling your organization on AI?
2. What is your recipe for selling AI?
3. What can you do to provide psychological safety for your team?

In 2024, a former student of Mark's saw an opportunity. She'd always been interested in technological change, especially using innovation to enhance the quality of life for the people in her community, and in her position as an innovation leader in her municipal government, she thought there could be potential to help improve government performance by leveraging the power of AI.

Some of her colleagues were excited, others were more cautious. The concerns centered on having the foundational AI skills, data privacy, and cybersecurity. IT wanted to make sure they had the technical and financial bandwidth to support AI adoption within their organization. The mayor, meanwhile, while believing in the power of innovation and curious about the potential benefits, was sensitive to the political risks associated with adopting a new and unproven technology.

Though her background was in computer science, Mark's student knew she would need to become half saleswoman, half negotiator to win over the hearts and minds of her colleagues. Her starting point was a recognition that several key players in leadership were not supporters, and some were even actively opposed. For AI to be successful, their buy-in was important. She also understood that the road to AI-land was long and had multiple steps, sometimes one step forward and two steps back. Being somewhat risk averse herself when it comes to her job, she wanted to start small and let small wins beget larger ones.

As a negotiator, she focused first on aligning a proposed AI initiative with the mayor's goals. Meeting with him, she laid out a vision of an AI-empowered organization, highlighting the benefits and bringing it to life by describing a day in the life of the public works department in an AI-supported world. Next, she leveraged the current budget crisis to frame AI as a means of maintaining constituent services at a lower cost. The urgency of budget action translated into urgency for AI. She also knew that a handful of department managers *had* been experimenting with generative AI and were eager to pilot applications, so she identified four who were AI enthusiasts to be her "customers" for a first initiative. She was confident that if they had success, others would follow.

Recognizing that fear is a major roadblock to any new initiative, she adopted a number of techniques to quell the concerns of her colleagues. She acknowledged the risks, but offered strategies to mitigate them—tackling the loss of competency by overemphasizing training those impacted by AI, for example. She tackled reactance, that immediate response of "no," with co-design. She thought about how she could get everyone to see the big-picture value of AI and invited department heads and their subject matter experts to identify and prioritize AI use cases. Rather than telling them how to adopt AI, she put herself in the role of mere process facilitator and scribe rather than primary proponent—leading the horses to water, but allowing them to decide how to take their drink.

She created psychological safety by having the mayor pledge that AI was a judgment-free zone. That is, the role of city officials was to test, learn, then test again. The final ingredient in her recipe was to use social proof to persuade the skeptics to join in. She enlisted local private sector companies that were successfully using AI to come explain their journeys. She did the same with AI uses in other cities. Finally, she tapped into the academic community to provide process expertise. The road was long and required a variety of nuanced tactics, but with all the ingredients in the mix, she was able to combine them to sell even the skeptics on trying AI.

If you're still reading this book after seven chapters, you likely see the potential for AI in your organization, but much like Mark's former student, you may be wondering whether your colleagues will recognize the same opportunity. If technological adoption is to work, a necessary condition for success is that your coworkers up and down your organization embrace AI. This will come when your leadership teams see how AI can align with your department's overall strategy and are willing to invest resources (money, time, political capital) to make it happen. You also need the buy-in of the people whose lives will change once you implement AI. They need to see that this new technology will improve their work life: eliminating drudgery, improving the quality of their decision-making, or providing them with greater schedule predictability. Equally important, they need to know that if AI replaces them, they still have a future—one that is attainable and positive.

Since we know what the endgame looks like, what is the recipe to get there? There is likely no single approach that you can use to win over the hearts and minds of your organization, but in this chapter, we provide a set of methodologies and frameworks that you can use to build your own recipe. Context always matters and it certainly does in selling change. The next section provides three guiding principles to help you bring your teams along as you work to make your organization better. The remainder of the chapter describes the various frameworks: what they are, when they are effective, and how to use them. Your job will be to decide which ones to use and how to combine them.

What are the barriers you envision to selling your organization on AI?

Guiding Principles

The United States in the early 1900s was in the midst of massive transformation. Model Ts chugged down the street, replacing the horses that had been ubiquitous since colonial times. Telephones were facilitating communications with family, friends, and business associates down the block and across the country. Electricity was lighting up homes and offering companies the ability to run their factories longer. And in 1911, businessman Charles Ranlett Flint invited the leaders of three data-driven companies—the International Time Recording Company, the Computing Scale Company, and the Tabulating Machine Company—to his office, where he convinced them that if they merged, their product set would be able to provide incredible value to businesses everywhere.

With the stakeholders on board, he established a holding company to control the three firms and moved its headquarters to Endicott, New York. Soon, their leading product was a tabulating machine originally designed to help the US Census Bureau collect data on the country's expanding population. Within less than a decade, revenue had doubled, largely thanks to sales of the tabulating machine, and the holding company took on a new name: International Business Machines, or IBM.

Despite this early growth, had IBM been content to rest its success on their once-popular tabulating machine, you would likely not know their acronym today. Instead, the company has survived for over a century by placing a huge priority on change. Not only is it the largest industrial research organization in the world—with nineteen research facilities across a dozen countries—but for twenty-nine consecutive years from 1993 to 2021, it held the record for most annual US patents.[1] It's thanks to IBM that we have ATMs, floppy disks, magnetic strip cards, and barcodes, and their employees have won a collective six Nobel Prizes and six Turing Awards (for technical innovation in computer science) for their work.

It is because of IBM that AI even exists. In 1956, one of their scientists named Arthur Samuel demonstrated the first practical example of artificial intelligence when he programmed an IBM 704 computer to not only play checkers but to "learn" from its past experience. Then in 2011, the company brought AI into the public consciousness when its Watson program defeated *Jeopardy!* champions Ken Jennings and Brad Rutter.

In contrast, history is littered with companies like Kodak, Blockbuster, and Digital Equipment that failed to think about the future. Sometimes, their lack of change came from failing to see disruptive innovation, such as Kodak hoping that digital photography, which it developed, would go away. On other occasions, egos got in the way, like when Blockbuster's CEO was so confident in his business model that he failed to see how Netflix could eliminate the need for brick-and-mortar movie stores. Yet another problem is the success trap, which befell Digital Equipment, when it was making so much money from its minicomputer business it ignored the personal computer market.

Unfortunately, failure to change is also evident in the public sector. Mark has spent much of his career working with freight railroads to improve their performance. When he began his career, American railroads were badly broken. The primary culprit was the Interstate Commerce Commission (ICC), the first federal government regulator, established in 1887. The ICC failed to change its regulatory approach despite the advent of automobiles, trucks, and aircraft. Each innovation reduced the viability of the railroads until in the 1980s the industry was in such bad shape that a stationary locomotive fell over on its side as the track under it gave way. The solution, decades too late, was to eliminate the ICC, which was done in 1996.

There is no denying it: change is hard, and it can be tempting to sit back and stick with what works well enough now instead of asking what opportunities there are to improve in the future. Unfortunately, though, not changing can be fatal, or leave an organization in the dust compared to its peers. Embracing AI is predicated on embracing change, so we need to adopt an IBM mindset within our own organizations. For example, "I am excited, or at least, willing to have an AI model scan resumes for promising candidates." Or, "delegating routine questions to a chatbot will be more responsive to constituent needs." Therefore, our task is to raise awareness of the need for change, communicate that message, and help the rest of the organization get on board. The following three principles provide a foundation for selling change.

Principle #1: Change Is an Unnatural Act

Think about the last time your cellphone was updated. Did you find yourself wondering: Where is my contact list? What happened to my favorite app? Notwithstanding the trivial nature of these changes, they are still frustrating. Now consider a hospital transitioning from a paper-based patient administration system to a digital one. Here the stakes are much higher, as is the aggravation level, since you need to train hundreds of people on how to use the system properly, with the risk of files being deleted or misassigned being a matter of literally life or death to patients. A dominant reason for resisting change is fear. Fear of the unknown: "What will this change mean for me?" Fear of loss: "People rely on me for that expertise." Fear of failure: "Will I be able to learn the new systems?"

The fear is stoked by our comfort with established routines. Changing habits requires effort and motivation. Lack of understanding the need for change also creates anxiety. "Why do I need to change?" "Will there be enough training?" The result is sticking with the status quo, that is, the path of least resistance. In professional settings, this manifests itself as "stay calm, hunker down and this too shall pass." Think about change in your organization. How many times have people just waited out a new directive until its champion gave up or was transferred?

Principle #2: Change Management Is a Process

There is no magic wand to make change happen. But there is a process that increases the probability of success. The process begins with preparation. Build the case for change. Describe the benefits, costs, risks, and return on investment. (Change always involves investment of budget, time, political capital, etc.) Also, understand who gains, who loses, and the emotions that will surround the change. Develop responses to the most difficult questions. Often these questions will be driven by fear: "What will happen to my job and job security?" "Will this make my work more difficult?" "Will it negatively impact our clients?" "Will I be held responsible when things beyond my control go wrong?" "Where do I begin to understand and apply these often-complex new tools?"

Next is the communications plan. Start with the content; what information needs to be shared to build trust and support for the change? Next, how will you package and deliver the information? What is the most effective way for people to see the value of change and how they are protected? Also, who are the best individuals to deliver the message? The communications are all about winning hearts and minds. Remember: emotions are more powerful than numbers. Making the messages about people is the best path to emotional support. Messages that link to people's interests are the most powerful.

Support and reinforcement are the final stages of the process. Support includes training on the new policies, processes, and/or technology. Perhaps more important and often overlooked is emotional support. The fears described in Principle 1 need to be addressed. Emotional support can ease anxiety. The support needs to be ongoing. One and done will not work. Even once the change is in place, you'll need to listen to those impacted by the change. Hear what is working and what is not. Make changes to improve substantive performance and emotional well-being.

Principle #3: Crawl, Walk, Run

You will not eliminate the fear and uncertainty about bringing AI into your organization with even the best communications plan. As Jerry Maguire said in the film of the same name: "Show me the money." Building momentum for "AI-ing" your organization comes from demonstrating that the words and plans match the reality. Starting with a pilot to learn how to embed AI into the fabric of the organization increases the probability of success. Let success beget successes.

Everett Rogers, the father of the S-Shaped adoption curve, provides guidance in the process of moving from crawling to walking to running. He argues that you need a few innovators and early adopters in the organization to try an innovation. Perhaps the head of human resources (HR) might use AI to help develop individualized training plans for employees. HR then becomes a champion of AI and helps sell it to others. This engages the early majority. They are the 30 percent of the organization that are open-minded and willing to change . . . assuming someone else did it first successfully. If the early majority buys in (the head of Public Works uses AI for identifying road quality and the head of Public Safety uses AI to determine EMT staffing, and the treasurer uses AI to answer constituent questions with a chatbot), the accumulated success brings on the late majority and with them AI becomes "how we do business."

Methodologies/Frameworks for Selling Change

Change management has been studied extensively by academics and practitioners. In this section, we offer a description of our favorite methodologies and frameworks. The best change plans are those that are custom designed, incorporating the elements of several frameworks that best address your context. Based on our experience working with policymakers over the years and what we know about AI in particular, we highlight a subset of methodologies here:

- Kotter's Leading Change;
- Adaptive Leadership;
- Human Element;
- Choice Architecture;
- Psychological Safety;
- Persuasion.

Certainly there are many others out there, and if you know of any that work for you, do use them! But this initial list offers a starting toolkit to help you win the hearts and minds of your colleagues when it comes to AI adoption (and anything else).

Kotter's Leading Change

We begin with Leading Change, developed by John Kotter of Harvard Business School (see Figure 8.1). Kotter provides a holistic view of the change process—from creating a sense of urgency and enlisting a guiding coalition of champions to articulating a strategy, generating quick wins, and institutionalizing the change. In selling your organization on AI, his suggestions regarding urgency are especially relevant. Many people might push off the adoption of AI, saying it is too early and uncertain, but there are a number of good arguments for conveying the need for testing AI. As we have pointed out throughout this book, AI is already in use in many, many areas of our lives,

KOTTER'S LEADING CHANGE

1. Create a Sense of Urgency
2. Build a Guiding Coalition
3. Form a Strategic Vision and Initiatives
4. Enlist a Volunteer Army
5. Enable Action by Removing Barriers
6. Generate Short-Term Wins
7. Sustain Acceleration
8. Institute Change

Figure 8.1 Kotter's leading change. Adapted from Kotter International Inc., "The 8 Steps for Leading Change," https://www.kotterinc.com/methodology/8-steps/

and AI resources do not need to be a big, scary giant tool—but can be used strategically to tackle some very targeted tasks effectively.

AI can potentially help address the challenges of an overworked and understaffed public service, and examples abound of AI drastically reducing the time needed to accomplish many tasks—sometimes by as much as 90, 95, or even 99 percent. Studies show that the time savings allow employees to focus on more engaging, strategic, and meaningful activities, resulting in enhanced employee fulfillment and client satisfaction.[2] As AI becomes increasingly familiar in our personal and professional lives, employees are starting to envision ways that it will help their careers and open up new employment opportunities.[3]

A second aspect of the Kotter model is the need for a clear vision of how the change aligns with the organization's goals, similar to how Mark's former student aligned the benefits AI could bring to her city with the mayor's own priorities and the pressing budget crisis. It's likely that explaining how AI can address budget constraints or workforce vacancies would be appropriate and relevant "hooks" for many government agencies. Tying into priorities provides the rationale for devoting time and resources to support AI use cases. The articulation of the vision becomes the communication vehicle to explain the "what" and "why" of using AI.

A third important element is enlisting champions, like the "customers" Mark's student found who, of their own accord, were already exploring AI tools. You will not be able to bring AI into your organization by yourself. This idea ties to Rogers' work on the S-shaped adoption curve. He found that two groups of people spurred adoption of change. The first group is opinion leaders. Every organization has those people who if you have a question, they have a valuable perspective to offer or if you are trying to understand where the organization is heading, they know. They are trusted and insightful. These are the people who will convince the early adopters and early majority to try AI. Rogers' second group is the external change agents. They influence the organization's decision-makers with their outside perspective and ability to operate without the constraints of the internal hierarchy and bureaucracy. To build support for its self-driving vehicles, for example, Waymo has enlisted the help of many influential organizations such as Mothers Against Drunk Driving, the National Safety Council, and the Blinded Veterans Association.

Adaptive Leadership

Understanding fear and loss is essential to overcoming resistance to change. This is especially true for AI, where the future is uncertain and there is no end of doomsday forecasts. Adaptive Leadership zeroes in on how human emotions are a barrier to change and how they can be overcome in uncertain environments. The dominant emotion associated with change is fear of loss. AI creates the potential for three types of losses (see Figure 8.2). Material loss, at the extreme, is the loss of your job. While this may be a low probability, it might create a fight-or-flight reaction. Flight is ignoring change and hoping it will go away or even leaving your job. Fight is "Hell no, I am not letting AI replace me!" The second type is loss of competency. "I know how to do my job and do it well. I don't know how to design and use an AI chatbot." The third

TYPES OF LOSSES WITH CHANGE

Material Loss: *I could lose my job if this change is implemented.*

Competency Loss: *I am really good a what I do today; this change means I will need to start all over.*

Connection Loss: *I like the interaction I have today; I will be isolated after the change.*

Adapted from Ronald A. Heifetz and Marty Linsky, *Leadership on the Line: Staying Alive Through the Dangers of Change* (Harvard Business Review Press: 2017)

Figure 8.2 Types of losses with change. Adapted from Ronald A. Heifetz and Marty Linsky, Leadership on the Lines: Staying Alive *Through the Dangers of Change* (Harvard Business Review Press: 2017).

type of loss is loss of connection. Most people enjoy the connection they have with others. "If my colleagues are replaced with an AI algorithm, who will I eat lunch with?" Taken together, these three types of losses show that adopting AI raises concerns about stability, identity, and belonging for your colleagues.

You can take several actions to minimize fear and loss. First is acknowledging the emotions. Be upfront about the concerns and give your colleagues that space to share their feelings. As they say in the world of psychology, you have to name it to tame it. Fear is most powerful when there is a lack of information. Therefore, the second action is involving those impacted by AI initiatives in the design, development, implementation, and evaluation of the system as Mark's former student did by allowing her colleagues to be the ones to identify their own potential use cases. Adaptive leadership talks about moving from the dance floor to the balcony. Most people are on the dance floor. They have an intimate understanding of their world and how it works. Moving to the balcony enables the team to see the big picture—in this case, how AI interacts with the organization as a whole.

The leadership team at Albert by Zoom, a company that leverages AI to help marketers make better advertising decisions, recognized that in order to win over skeptics, their best bet was to show them the big picture. To that end, they developed a visualization tool called Inside Albert that provided advertisers with a holistic picture of the thousands of microsegments their system was creating and their performance levels. While employees had initially been critical of the platform for failing to fully take advantage of what teams had previously found were their best-performing attributes and frequencies, Inside Albert's visualizations helped them realize that the platform was finding new markets through its ability to microsegment to a degree not previously possible.[4]

A third action is explicitly addressing the three types of losses. Provide employment protection, in current jobs or with new ones. (Let attrition work to reap the efficiency gains of AI.) Include in the implementation design enough training to overcome the competency worry. Finally, replace the loss of connective tissue in the organization. At one end of the spectrum are social interactions such as team lunches. At the other end is a reorganization post-AI implementation that creates new teams.

Think about the last time you bought furniture for your home. We suspect you experienced a range of emotions during the purchase process. There was probably the salesperson who told you about all the benefits of replacing your current furniture and the wonderful attributes of your potential purchase. If you hesitated, the salesperson pointed out more features of the new furniture and perhaps lowered the price to get you to say, "I'll buy it."

Human Element

Now think about why you hesitated. Was it concerns about the benefits? Probably not. Rather, it was concerns about the possible losses associated with the purchase. Will I have buyer's remorse? Will it be too big for the space? What will I do with the old furniture? Would I rather use the money for a vacation? These questions are collectively known as the human element of change. Nordgren and Schonthal, who wrote a book called *The Human Element: Overcoming the Resistance That Awaits New Ideas*, suggest the "progressive fuel" (the benefits) are overshadowed by the "aversive fuel" (the concerns). The concerns related to change are (1) inertia—too overwhelming, (2) effort—too much work and an unclear plan, (3) emotion—risk of loss, and (4) reactance—a violation of my beliefs (see Figure 8.3).

You overcome inertia by starting small and demonstrating that the change is done in bite-sized chunks. A powerful complement is having an internal opinion leader or external change agent attest to the feasibility of the proposed AI system. The effort barrier is overcome with a clear road map, simple steps, and sufficient resources to get the job done right. We suggested strategies to address loss aversion in the adaptive leadership section above.

OVERCOMING THE "HUMAN ELEMENT"

Inertia	**Effort**
• Repetition	• Road Map
• Start Small	• Streamline/Simplify
• Find a Familiar Face	• Make it the Default
• Make it Relative	• Reduce the Load
• Show an Extreme	

Emotion	**Reactance**
• Focus on Why	• Know What is Core
• Be an Ethnographer	• Ask Don't Tell
• Bring the Outside In	• Co-Design

Adapted from Loran Nordgren and David Schonthal, *The Human Element: Overcoming the Resistance That Awaits New Ideas* (Wiley: 2022) https://www.humanelementbook.com

Figure 8.3 Overcoming the "human element." Adapted from Loran Nordgren and Davi Schonthal, *The Human Element: Overcoming the Resistance That Awaits New Ideas* (Wiley: 2022), https://www.humanelementbook.com

Reactance is the most challenging aversive fuel to overcome. Reactance is defined as an emotional reaction to pressure to change that actually increases the opposition to the change. Three actions can reduce reactance. Know what is core to the people who are being asked to change. The more core to their beliefs, the more difficult it is for people to change. Thus, knowing what is core prevents inadvertently triggering a negative response. *Asking* people to change is much more effective at reducing reactance than telling the team that they *must* change. Third, where possible, co-design the change. Psychologists tell us that participation provides a sense of agency and control and reduces reactance.

Choice Architecture

Another tool for changing behavior is choice architecture, commonly known as nudges. If you want more people to save for retirement, enroll new employees in the retirement plan as the default. They can opt out if they want but extensive research shows they will not. This is the essence of choice architecture or nudging people to behave in a desired way. The nudges can be a function of placement (put the fruit before the desserts in the school cafeteria line), pricing (sin taxes) or promotion (what you emphasize). When it comes to selling AI, consider priming. Sharing stories of successes at other organizations, comparing AI to internal changes that went well, and frequent reinforcement of this messaging can improve the receptivity of the organization.

In 2023, Mary Callahan Erdoes, CEO of the asset and wealth management division of JPMorganChase, attended a talk on AI that was so impactful she wanted every member of her leadership team to think about how AI could and would change their operations. Since then, she has spent a significant amount of time reinforcing this message, including literally sending her team to conferences and events focused on AI—including bringing twenty-two of her people to the 2024 Harvard Business School's "Leading With AI" conference.

Psychological Safety

A necessary condition for selling change is psychological safety. People who are psychologically safe will share their true thoughts, be willing to take risks, and not fear failure. These are essential ingredients for adopting AI. There is risk. We need people to share negative perspectives to stave off problems.

PSYCHOLOGICAL SAFETY

Learner Safety	Collaborator Safety
I am comfortable:	**I am comfortable:**
• Asking Questions	• Interacting with Colleagues
• Experimenting	• Fostering Debate
• Learning from Mistakes	• Establishing and
• Looking for New Solutions	Maintaining an Open Dialog

Challenger Safety	Inclusion Safety
I am comfortable:	**I feel:**
• Questioning the Status Quo	• Valued
• Questioning Authority	• Everyone is Treated Fairly
• Speaking Up	• Everyone's Opinions
• Exposing Problems	are Valued

Adapted from Sara King, "How and Why to Create Safety Within Your Teams," World Wide Technology, November 9, 2020, https://www.wwt.com/article/how-and-why-to-create-safety-within-your-teams

Figure 8.4 Psychological safety. Adapted from Sara King, "How and Why to Create Safety Within Your Teams," World Wide Technology, November 9, 2020, https://www.wwt.com/article/how-and-why-to-create-safety-within-your-teams

There may be failures. If there are negative consequences associated with the failure, no one will take risks. There are four dimensions of safety: learner, challenger, collaborator, and inclusion (see Figure 8.4). Learner safety enables people to ask difficult questions, experiment, and learn from mistakes. Challenger safety permits people to question the status quo, expose problems, and offer countervailing views. Safety regarding collaboration allows for extensive interaction within and outside the organization. Treating people fairly and helping them feel that their perspectives matter are elements of inclusion safety.

The starting point for establishing psychological safety is communicating its principles to the group and then walking the talk. Proactively encourage participation by all stakeholders, even the annoying ones. Reward candor and praise prudent risk-taking. Assign individuals to be the skeptics. Focus on learning from failure, not on the failure itself. In selling AI, provide safe spaces for experimentation and mistakes using pilots and sandboxes.

What can you do to provide psychological safety for your team?

Persuasion

A final framework to support your selling AI is old-fashioned persuasion. There is a long list of persuasion experts. Our favorite is Robert Cialdini, who describes six actions that can be combined to make a powerful sell. He begins with reciprocity: "You help me and I will help you." In experiments, he finds that when you offer support to others, they return the favor and provide even greater support: "You help me sell the organization on AI and I will help you with the new finance system." Next is consistency. The sell must be consistent with past history and with people's core values. We do not trust flip-floppers. Adopting a chatbot with an agreement not to downsize the current workforce but following this with layoffs will undermine any future attempts to adopt AI.

> **What is your recipe for selling AI?**
>
> ____
>
> ____
>
> ____
>
> ____

Cialdini's third action is liking. Not surprisingly, people are more able to be persuaded by people they like. Mark often thinks about who is the best messenger for change recommendations. It is often not him as the outside consultant. Rather, it is someone who is an internal option leader. A fourth persuasion tool is authority. We are influenced by those in authority. Think about advertisements for lawyers; they typically feature images of books and a flag in the background to persuade you that they are authority figures who can and therefore should be trusted. In selling AI to an organization, the authority can come from external experts. An extreme would be having Sam Altman of OpenAI help you pitch the need for AI.

The last two persuasion tools are social proof and scarcity. For selling sneakers, a professional basketball player is the right image. A line outside a restaurant is social proof that the food is good. Social proof also comes in the form of organizations that have successfully adopted the AI résumé screening algorithm you are proposing. Their success reduces the risk for your group. Think about the last time you were online buying an airline ticket. You might recall seeing the yellow highlighted banner claiming "only 1 seat left at this price." This is persuasion through scarcity. The fear of buying is replaced by the fear of missing out on this great deal. It works. In the world of AI, scarcity can come in offers for free system development in exchange for being a beta test site.

Having now seen this approach in action through a real-world example, the next step is for you to start putting the pieces together in your own organization, which is the purpose of Part III. Before turning the page, reflect on the insights from this chapter.

Write the key insights you take from the chapter and how it is relevant to bringing AI into your organization.

Part III

Getting Started

Chapter 9: Identifying and Prioritizing Use Cases

- Instead of rushing into AI, organizations should try a more problem/opportunity-centered approach to identifying and prioritizing use cases. Understand AI, pain points, and/or opportunities; assess if AI is an option; and then determine if AI is the best option.

- While AI is especially effective for generating time savings for internal staff or constituents, and for searching and translating, there are also challenges—politics, procurement process, multiple customers, and endless opportunities. Thus, the need for a framework to identify and prioritize AI use cases.

- A six-step process leads to the right AI use cases and priorities; it starts with profiling the core processes of the organization and ends with designing and running a pilot program using AI.

Chapter 10: Applying the Framework to the Judicial Courts

- As an example of AI tools in practice, this chapter offers a hypothetical example of how the framework for identifying and prioritizing AI use cases could be applied to the judicial courts.

- The selection of the courts is intentional, as it is an example where the potential benefits are high, but the risks of using AI are also high. It is also an area where AI is being used and a familiar topic for many. Moreover, the operation of the court system has two core streams of activity, the administration of the courts and legal decision-making.

- Organization leaders should ask themselves about the parallels between the use of AI in the courts and the use of AI in their own organization. This example illustrates how to think through the application of the AI use case identification and prioritization framework in a real-world environment.

Chapter 11: Beginning with Generative AI

- Using generative AI offers organizations a fast path forward. Starting with common tasks such as drafting reports, summarizing feedback, or translating content allows an agency to build internal familiarity with AI while delivering immediate benefits in efficiency and service delivery.

- The "crawl, walk, run" approach allows organizations to begin with off-the-shelf tools and progress toward more tailored solutions as capacity grows.

- Responsible deployment requires clear governance, strong privacy protections, and ongoing evaluation of efficiency, accuracy, and user adoption. Thoughtful implementation of generative AI can improve service quality, reduce administrative burden, and strengthen the relationship between governments and the people they serve.

Chapter 9

Identifying and Prioritizing Use Cases

Chapter Summary

AI is headline news and there is a temptation to implement this new technology as quickly as possible. We suggest a more problem/opportunity-centered approach. Understand AI, pain points and/or opportunities; assess if AI is an option; and then determine if AI is the best option. AI is especially effective for generating time savings for internal staff or constituents—think of facial recognition at Passport Control. AI is also effective for searching. If you need to find twenty data elements in a 1,000-page document, AI will do it fast and accurately. Increasingly, AI is an effective translator. Many government agencies serve constituents with multiple languages. AI can provide reliable, fast, and low-cost translations. There are of course the challenges—politics, procurement process, multiple customers, and endless opportunities. Thus, a framework is needed to identify and prioritize AI use cases.

A six-step process leads to the right AI use cases and priorities. Step 1 is profiling the core processes of the organization. What are they and how well do they work today? Step 2 is to formally assess the processes and categorize them into green ("all good"), yellow ("OK but could be better"), and red ("this is a problem or opportunity"). The reds are then prioritized based on impact on the organization/constituents and the ability to change the process. Identifying AI applications that can address the red is Step 3. Are applications being used today? Are they working well? Since we want you to keep your job, we want to keep you off the "bleeding" edge. Step 4 is determining if AI is the best solution, considering the costs and benefits of AI or alternatives. Step 5 is prioritizing the AI use cases and creating a roadmap for implementation. Finally, Step 6 is designing and running a pilot program using AI.

Learning Questions and Food for Thought

1. Based on what you have read so far and your own exposure to AI, what are the potential use cases for your organization?
2. What processes are most problematic and/or offer the best opportunity for improvement?
3. What do you think are the high-priority reds?
4. Who do you need to engage with to identify and prioritize the AI uses cases?

According to historical records, the first tax collection system established in what is today Spain was set up by the Romans, about 2,500 years ago. You might think that with such ancient origins, the country's present-day national tax agency would be slow to adapt to change—but that is not the case. In fact, the Agencia Tributaria (Spanish Tax Agency) was one of the first government departments in the world to produce an AI strategy document, to ensure they understood the potential and concerns of this cutting-edge technology and could use it strategically and effectively to improve their work.

The Agencia's policymakers believe AI can make their agency better, but recognize new technology is not a panacea and that—as we've discussed in previous chapters—without thoughtful application, these products can cause more problems than they solve. The department's agents have committed themselves to applying AI responsibly, ethically, and using a human-centric approach that provides full transparency to stakeholders. It is imperative that Spanish citizens trust their tax collection agency, so in their strategy document the agency also outlines where AI will *not* be used—such as in tax inspections. Following their own guidelines, the tax agency has been able to thoughtfully and strategically implement AI tools, most notably through a partnership with IBM that enables Spaniards to use the Watson AI platform to answer questions about value-added taxes. This has led to an 80 percent reduction in email inquiries to the tax authority, as Watson has been able to effectively address the vast majority of user inquiries.[1]

A former program director for digital transformation in the Office of Public Prosecutions in Victoria, Australia, argues that while AI is clearly generating headlines, policymakers want to be cautious that in a rush to implement new technology in their own departments, they are not adopting a solution in search of a problem. As with any area of your operations, it is important to see where the challenges lie, then explore possible solutions—some of which might use AI, either primarily or as a complement to a broader solution set. It can be tempting to want to dive in immediately, but it is most prudent to instead follow the lead of the Agencia Tributaria and understand AI first, and then as you identify problems, assess whether an AI platform would be appropriate. After all, AI is not a "set it and forget it" solution. An AI tool like a chatbot can cost in the $50,000-$100,000 range[2] and will require technical expertise, systems integration, and process changes to operate—so you want to be thoughtful in any implementation process.

Listening to various media reports, you might conclude that "AI everything" is just around the corner; however, the US Census Bureau has found that as of 2023 only four percent of businesses were using AI to produce goods and services. Even in the information sector, the heaviest adopters, the number was just under 14 percent.[3] So this technology is still in its infancy. We do not think it necessary for managers of scarce government resources to be on the leading (i.e., the "bleeding") edge of these new tools. Instead, once we know where the problems lie, much like Spain's tax agency, we can find an established, targeted tool to address them. In this chapter, we lay out a process for assessing problems and determining whether AI can be an appropriate part of a solution.

AI: What Is It Good For?

Time Savings

Are you familiar with queuing theory—the study of waiting in lines? If there is one insight queuing theory has taught us, it is that (as you probably know from your own life experiences), people do not enjoy being stuck in a queue. As policymakers, anything we can do to reduce the amount of time our stakeholders need to wait is positive, and AI technology can be most effective in this regard in a number of ways.

There might be no place more hated for a long wait than an airport, as travelers anxiously wait to get through security, ever worried they might miss their flight. In Narita Airport in Japan, though, facial recognition software has made the whole process much smoother. Face Express identifies passengers via a photo image at their first touchpoint at the airport, enabling them to pass through the rest of the airport without interruption, while advanced robotics detect anomalies about people, baggage, and equipment.[4] Beyond just detecting baggage, AI has the ability to sense emotions based on training data, which can be used to detect suspicious activity. AI systems have been trained based on facial and voice recognition as well as text to identify human emotions, from happiness and sadness to anger and anxiety. Security personnel can use this information to detect suspicious activity, but emotion detection is also useful for a range of other applications, such as predicting mental health concerns and providing proactive interventions.

On the phone or online, Americans also hate having to wait to connect with a customer service representative, but AI cuts back on these frustrations by interactively answering questions. AI chatbots have the ability to allow you to ask (via voice or text) a question and get a custom response to your specific concern, in a matter of seconds. These systems also allow you to refine your ask based on the response. For example, you might have the following exchange with a school department chatbot:

- You: "What documents do I need to register my child for school?"
- AI: Proof of address such as a utility bill.
- You: "I don't pay the utilities."
- AI: You can also use a letter from the city government mailed to your name and address.

The results are fast and responsive information, 24/7/365, for the constituent and a lower cost for the school department. The interaction can happen in literally dozens of languages. These chatbots do not even just answer questions but can also direct users effectively; the Rwandan government, for example, worked with Babylon Health to create chatbots capable of assisting the triage process for patients calling the hospital. Upon hearing the callers' symptoms, the triage tool would provide recommendations for accessing care.[5]

Searching

You might be old enough to recall an age when most books or documents were only available in print, and how time-consuming it could be to find a specific word or phrase in the text. If you were lucky there was an index that could guide you, but if not, you had no choice but to go through the whole book, searching for the relevant words yourself. The advent of a digital "search" function has saved us all an incredible amount of time, but even still, if you want to find synonyms you still need to enter each word yourself. AI takes searching to a new level, able to track down synonyms, antonyms, or other linguistic combinations quickly and effectively. Besides searching and finding, AI uses Large Language Models (LLMs) to draw from the entire internet to query information. They are also effective in synthesizing vast amounts of data and turning it into useful information. As an example of these processes, the US Veterans Administration is using AI to synthesize veteran feedback on the agency's services to identify performance trends and issues for detailed analysis.

On a more macro level, heat is the leading weather-related killer in the United States, so the National Oceanic and Atmospheric Administration wanted to determine heat-island locations in order to implement proactive responses to reduce the negative effects of excessive heat.[6] Enter AI, because AI systems are highly effective at finding patterns in numerical data or text, without bias and in much higher volumes than humans. AI anomaly identification capabilities are helping to provide security at airports like Narita, identify traffic bottlenecks, and predict disease outbreaks. AI systems are also used to identify and predict malfunctions and faults such as weakness in infrastructure or impending failure of machinery, and the US Patent and Trademark Office is using AI to search for materials that help determine the current state of the art as it evaluates patent applications.[7]

Accurate forecasts are the foundation for many services, from predicting storms and managing traffic to operating the electric grid and predicting health outcomes for individual patients. Predicting electricity production is illustrative. The AI algorithm integrates historical production trends, operational efficiency, weather forecasts, and weather conditions at a very detailed level to estimate the amount of electricity that will be needed and the optimal portfolio for generation. The better the prediction, the more reliable the electric grid.[8]

Language

Need a birthday message for a friend? Need an op-ed? Need a training manual? LLMs are your solution. Enter a few prompts and out comes the text in seconds. Need to make it easier to understand? Prompt the program to write for an eighth grader and it is produced in seconds. Not only can AI write, but it can also write in multiple languages.

These are the areas where AI programs excel, though this list is not exhaustive as new AI capabilities are increasing daily:

- Sensing emotions and reading body language;

- Searching, finding, reading, and summarizing;

- Writing prose;

- Answering questions interactively;

- Recognizing patterns and anomalies;

- Integrating multiple inputs and projecting outcomes.

AI offers many opportunities, but as a public sector manager, you face several unique challenges that impact the use case selection. The first is that AI decisions have a political overlay. Operational objectives must be combined with political realities in identifying viable use cases. Using an AI hiring algorithm may create a risk of bias that is greater than a city mayor is willing to accept. A corollary factor is general risk aversion. Media and public scrutiny may limit risk-taking. Neither the governor nor the cabinet secretary is willing to lose their job because of an AI implementation gone bad.

A second concern for public organizations is the procurement process. Many government entities have strict purchasing rules that may dictate the selection of the low-cost supplier. If the low-cost provider is also the best-qualified supplier, the outcome is great. However, this is not always the case. Public procurement regulations also can limit collaboration with potential suppliers. AI is new and ever evolving. Close collaboration between the government and the provider is needed to modify specifications as the AI product is being developed and delivered. This is often challenging in the public sphere.

Managing multiple customers is another complexity faced as government organizations bring in AI. Who is the customer for a mental health AI product? Is the customer the recipient of the services? The person's family? Civil society? Each has their own interests. Determining how to simultaneously satisfy all needs can be so daunting that the status quo persists. Finally, there are endless opportunities. The range of AI use cases in government is broad and dense. This, combined with limited funds and expertise, elevates the need to carefully prioritize AI use cases. The next section provides a framework for identifying and prioritizing AI use cases.

> Based on what you have read so far and your own exposure to AI, what are the potential use cases for your organization?
>
> ____
>
> ____
>
> ____

The Framework

Have you ever been "hangry"—so hungry that you feel upset or even angry? It happens to the best of us, but sometimes the ramifications can be quite significant. In fact, in 2011, a group of researchers published a paper arguing that judges, as we all do, feel the effects of an empty stomach; but when they do, they are less likely to grant parole to an inmate.

In the study, the researchers looked at 1,000 parole decisions made by eight judges who heard between fourteen and thirty-five cases per day, separated into a morning session followed by a second session after a snack break, and ending with a third session starting after lunch and going until the end of the day. Every one of the eight judges followed the same pattern: they were much less likely to grant parole to a prisoner at the end of a session than at the beginning. In fact, if the judge heard your case at the beginning of their session, they were twice as likely to grant you parole than if you appeared in front of their bench just before they broke for a snack, lunch, or at the end of the day.[9]

In the decade and a half since the publication of the original study, other scholars (such as Lakens 2017 and Glöckner 2016) argue it is not specifically hunger that is leading to such discrepancies in case outcomes; nevertheless, the legal community does now recognize there are factors at play in parole and sentencing proceedings that might result in inmates being treated differently, even though the criminal justice system is built around the idea that we are all supposed to be treated equally. In an attempt to rectify this problem, court systems across the country in places like New York, Wisconsin, California, and Florida have adopted machine learning-based software designed to use large datasets to determine whether a specific inmate is at risk of reoffending, removing some of the bias from a (hungry) judge's hands.[10]

This case illustrates the process of identifying an existing problem and implementing an AI-based solution to address it. In this section, we will help you look at your own operations to emerge with a list of AI applications that will enhance the delivery of government services, especially those where

USE CASE IDENTIFICATION AND PRIORITIZATION FRAMEWORK

Step 1: Profile Sore Functions

Step 2: Prioritize "Reds" or Pain Points

Step 3: Identify AI Application for Top-Priority Reds

Step 4: Assess AI Solutions

Step 5: Prioritize AI Solutions

Step 6: Design and Run a Pilot

Figure 9.1 Use case identification and prioritization framework. Generated by the authors.

current performance is inadequate. Your list should also reflect the ability of your organization to successfully implement the AI use case at an appropriate level of risk.

The framework of six steps listed in Figure 9.1 is detailed below.

Step 1: Profile Core Functions

The starting point for identifying potential AI use cases is profiling the functions performed by your agency and highlighting the external and internal functions that are both critical and for which performance is not fully satisfactory. External functions are those providing service to constituents/customers. In the case of a state's registry of motor vehicles, for example, they include conducting driving permit exams and road tests, providing driver's licenses, transferring vehicle ownership titles, registering vehicles, certifying insurance coverage, and driver safety awareness. Internal functions range from hiring and developing staff to designing and implementing IT and operating service centers. As you conduct this exercise for your own organization, you should strive for a comprehensive list.

Next, map the functions based on criticality. A simple test of criticality is: Will managers be fired if the function is not readily available? This outcome is unlikely if a public safety campaign is delayed a few weeks, but likely if licenses cannot be issued for a few days. A more comprehensive approach involves four tasks. The first is to map stakeholder expectations: Who are the stakeholders and what do they want and expect, and how do these align by function? The second task is to assess the power and interest of the stakeholders, again by function. Power includes political influence, funding, expertise, and legitimacy. Interest is how much of a priority this is for the stakeholder. The third task is to map the criticality of the agency functions on a spectrum from critical to less important, based on the stakeholder assessment. The final task is to consider the margin of error associated with the task. Is the error tolerance associated with AI acceptable? Interestingly, in the case of AVs, human error (i.e., driver-caused crashes) is more acceptable than AI failures.

> What processes are most problematic and/or offer the best opportunity for improvement?
> ____
> ____
> ____
> ____

Step 2: Prioritize the "Reds"

Because resources are limited, you should prioritize the focus of adopting AI to the critical functions where there is significant room for improvement. A green/yellow/red performance assessment provides an easy-to-implement and communicate approach. Where possible, your assessment should be quantitative, using measures like wait times, processing times, and/or customer satisfaction surveys. Qualitative evidence will also be helpful, looking at elements like the number of positive versus negative ratings on Yelp-like sites. Input from your managers and employees also plays a role in the assessment. The green/yellow/red designation will be subjective, but having some measurements that define each is preferable where possible. The AI use case priorities are the most critical "reds" (see Figure 9.2 for an approach to mapping the criticality of "reds").

For many government services, different constituents/customers have different needs and expectations, so segmenting users can tease out nuances. In the registry example above, for instance, drivers who can renew their license online view wait times differently from those who need to complete the renewal in person. Geography can be another important way to segment. Those who live far from the registry are likely to have little tolerance for failing to complete their transaction in a single trip with minimal waiting time. Equity is also a consideration—for instance, having multilingual staff at some locations can be more important than at others.

CRITICALITY MAPPING OF THE TASK-LEVEL "REDS"

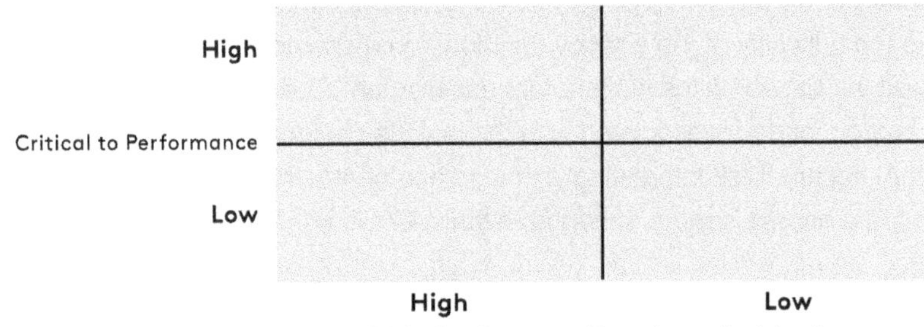

Figure 9.2 Criticality mapping of the task-level "reds". Generated by the authors.

What do you think are the high-priority reds?

Step 3: Identify AI Applications for Top-Priority Reds

AI is unlikely to be the solution to all the reds. There are functions where AI has a comparative advantage, yet others where you will likely find non-AI solutions are preferable. Also, there are applications where AI has a well-established track record and others where it is not ready for prime time. The risks of adopting AI can be reduced by being a fast follower rather than a first mover. Regulation is also a factor. In some geographies, higher-risk applications require extra scrutiny.

Another risk mitigation strategy is to segment the reds based on back-office versus customer/constituent-facing activities. Back-office activities are often lower risk. Also, less-critical functions may be a good starting point.[11] The counterpoint is that AI is a major undertaking, consuming funds, time, and expertise. Therefore, the use cases addressed need to generate enough value to ensure there is a strong positive return on investment.

Back-office or constituent-facing, the applications require data for training and testing. An additional screen is the availability of that data. Today that data might not be collected and ready for use. If you think about the long term, beginning to collect the data now might enable the effective use of AI in the future as new algorithms are developed.

A good starting point for identifying AI applications is seeing where AI is currently in use in the public sector. Beginning with existing applications ensures the use case works and provides the social proof that will be helpful in selling the idea to internal and external stakeholders. Moreover, the people running the existing applications can be a source of insight.

Focusing on existing public sector applications ensures the AI use is appropriate in the unique government context. The US federal government maintains an inventory of AI applications.[12] The list includes uses by twenty-seven federal departments and agencies, from Justice and State to the Environmental Protection Agency and the National Science Foundation. For example, the Department of Homeland Security's AI inventory includes applications for headquarters functions, as well as uses in the subagencies including the Transportation Security Administration (TSA), Federal Emergency Management Agency (FEMA), Customs and Border Protection (CBP), and the Cybersecurity and Infrastructure Security Agency (CISA). Use case examples include:

- Geospatial damage assessments (FEMA);

- AI for Autonomous Situational Awareness (CBP);

- Automated Indicator Sharing—Scoring and Feedback (CISA);

- Touchless Precheck Identity Solution (TSA).

Scanning the hundreds of current AI use cases serves as an effective thought-starter for addressing the "reds."

Another source of AI applications in the public sector is the Government AI Coalition initiated by the city of San Jose, California, in 2023. The mission of the coalition is to provide a vehicle for state and local government to have a voice in architecting the AI future.[13] The coalition includes representatives from 250 state, county, and local government organizations. The group's work is guided by the following goals:

- Use AI for social good;

- Ensure ethical, nondiscriminatory, and responsible AI governance;

- Promote vendor accountability;

- Improve government services; and

- Foster cross-agency collaboration and knowledge-sharing.

They offer a range of resources to support the development of AI tools, including use case templates and a registry of AI vendors.

Private sector AI applications offer another source of insight, especially where the application can be implemented in the public sector without extensive modification. AI use cases in the private sector cover the gamut of industries, from law and insurance to real estate, finance, and manufacturing. The use cases include:[14]

- Chatbots for customer service;
- Productivity tools, from scheduling and note-taking to performance assessment;
- Fraud detection and credit scoring in finance;
- Market analysis and predicting prices in purchasing;
- Quality assurance, predictive maintenance, and process automation in manufacturing;
- Research and records management in law; and
- Call centers in many sectors.

A third source is AI providers. We can segment the AI provider community into (1) solution providers; (2) AI-powered product providers; and (3) AI consultants/integration providers. The solution providers offer AI products that address specific functions and/or industries. OpenAI's ChatGPT and IBM's Watson are examples of products that offer solutions that cut across functions and industries. For example, Watson can be used to create chatbots, streamline coding, and find insights in datasets. AI-powered product providers like Apple (Siri) and Amazon (Alexa) use AI to support use cases including research, personal assistants, and managing the Internet of Things at home. A cadre of AI consulting firms offers services to help design and implement AI applications. Their comparative advantages are AI expertise and customization to the specific client needs.

Another source is open-source projects where developers create AI applications and make them available to the public. They are free and often have an extensive user base that continually improves the application. Examples run the gamut from productivity and coding to science and research. These offerings might not look pretty, but they can be an effective starting point.

While AI applications are not prevalent in all organizations, it is likely that someone is using AI to address your reds. Try using AI to find that needle in the haystack, but make sure you verify.

Step 4: Assess AI Solutions

As you have likely already guessed, just because an AI solution exists does not mean you adopt it. Like any initiative, AI applications must have a positive return on your investment and the benefits must outweigh the costs. The benefits include improvements in the quality, efficiency, and equity of services you provide to customers, but internal improvements in effectiveness and efficiency should also be part of your calculus.

You will need to consider a range of costs, including the money to acquire, implement, and maintain the system as well as the staff time to incorporate the AI application into existing operations. There are also the costs of having staff monitor the application, especially when you first implement it. Given the newness of the technology, the human intervention might last a long time. New data also adds to costs as more information has the potential to improve performance but also requires time to retrain and retest.

Change in general, and with AI in particular, introduces risks. These include operational risk, the costs resulting from the failure to deliver required services, and reputational risks if the AI implementation fails to meet your stakeholders' expectations. As mentioned above, these risks are greater in the public sector where failures are likely to be very visible. The media and political critics can easily amplify news of a failure, reinforcing the damage to your organization's reputation. An additional consideration is the capacity for AI change. Do you have the expertise to bring in a new application? Also, what other initiatives are crowded out by the AI adoption?

You need to quantify the costs and benefits as much as possible (see Figure 9.3). Many of the costs are comparatively easy to quantify. The funds paid to vendors are clear. If payments take place over time, they can be discounted to get a present-value cost. The time needed for training is also easily estimated, with a drop in productivity during a transition period. Risk will be harder to quantify. One approach is to look at the impact of other failures on your organization. For example, was your budget reduced when a failure took place? The risk assessment also needs to reflect the strength of the AI provider—reliability, responsiveness, expertise, bandwidth, and long-term financial viability.

COSTS AND BENEFITS CONSIDERATIONS

Cost Factors

Direct
- Development or Use Fees
- Operating and Maintenance
- Quality Control and Security

Indirect
- Change Management and Training

Benefit Factors

Direct
- Faster Provision
- Labor Savings & Constituent Savings
- High Resource Utilization

Indirect
- Constituent and/or Employee Satisfaction
- More Accurate and Equitable Outcomes

Risk Considerations
- Cost: Underestimate Cost and Time for Implementation
- Benefit: Overestimate Improvement Gains
- Understate Political Risks

Figure 9.3 Costs and benefits considerations. Generated by the authors.

Benefits are often more difficult to quantify. What is the value of a more responsive employee who has been hired based on an AI algorithm, for example? The following offers a segmentation and progression for quantifying benefits.

- **Segment 1: Direct Financial Gains**—If the AI application reduces staffing levels, the avoided labor costs are in the benefit set. Or if AI reduces raw material needs and space required, the eliminated expenses are included.

- **Segment 2: Improved Accuracy**—AI algorithms can often outperform humans. For example, AI programs are often better at detecting anomalies in medical imaging than humans.

- **Segment 3: Customer Time Savings**—Returning to the registry of motor vehicles example, if AI scheduling reduces average wait time by ten minutes per customer, the value of the time savings is estimated as a benefit. Time savings are routinely quantified for transportation infrastructure assessments. The cumulative time saved by all users is multiplied by an average wage rate to approximate the dollar amount of the benefits.

- **Segment 4: Ancillary Benefits**—Some gains from AI adoption are indirect. For example, an AI traffic model that reduces congestion not only saves time but also reduces carbon emissions. Protocols for quantifying carbon reduction benefits are now well established.

- **Segment 5: Reputational Gains**—AI-improved performance can improve an organization's reputation, leading to a variety of benefits, including increased budget, enhanced recruiting of desired candidates, and less stress for employees.

The focus of your cost and benefit analysis should be on quantitative data, but qualitative information can also be valuable. Descriptive narratives, especially of benefits, can often bring the benefits of AI to life. A customer who says they were able to get immediate and accurate help from a tax authority chatbot rather than wait on the phone for twenty minutes is powerful evidence of the value of AI.

There may be multiple AI options to address a specific red opportunity. In those cases, you should complete the benefit-cost analysis for each option, then choose the option with the best return on investment. In making this determination, consider the working relationship you will establish with the AI provider. You will be partners for a long time, so make sure you have the right "chemistry."

A final assessment is a make-buy decision. Should you develop and implement the AI application internally or partner with a third party? The assessment criteria include:

- Expertise;
- Cost;
- Time-to-use;
- Customization;
- Maintenance;
- Data protection;
- IP control.

Expertise, cost, and time are typically the threshold considerations. Where possible, quantify the assessment, but in most cases your final decision will be a qualitative one.

Step 5: Prioritize AI Solutions

You will complete the prior step for each of the top-priority reds. Before launching initiatives that have a strong positive benefit-cost analysis, develop a road map to the overall AI plan. AI applications need to fit into the overall strategy and system of the organization. An AI application that, for example, provides more accurate forecasts of demand is necessary but not sufficient to improve customer satisfaction unless it is accompanied by a delivery system that is agile enough to use the improved forecasts.

Create a road map of how to sequence the AI applications that address immediate needs, the reds. Divide the map into a near-term plan (two to twenty-four months) and a long-term view of two to four years. The sequencing should balance the comparative importance of the applications to performance with the risk-adjusted net benefits. Review and refine a draft mapping reflecting the organization's overall strategy.

Step 6: Design and Run a Pilot

Finally, complete this task by identifying one or two initiatives to adopt as a pilot, taking AI for a test drive in a low-stakes environment to learn what works and what does not. Those applications you select to pilot should have a high probability of success in light of the capabilities of the technology, the provider, and the implementing team. To bring this entire process to life, we go through a hypothetical example—applying the framework to the judicial courts—in Chapter 10.

> Write the key insights you take from the chapter and how it is relevant to bringing AI into your organization.
> ______________________________________
> ______________________________________
> ______________________________________
> ______________________________________

Fill in the key takeaways from this chapter below.

> Write the key insights you take from the chapter and how it is relevant to bringing AI into your organization.
> ______________________________________
> ______________________________________
> ______________________________________
> ______________________________________

Chapter 10

Applying the Framework to the Judicial Courts

Chapter Summary

This chapter illustrates how the AI use case identification and prioritization framework can be applied. The application is in the judicial courts. The selection of the courts is intentional. We want an example where the potential benefits are high, but the risks of using AI are also high. It is also an area where AI is being used and a topic that all of us have some level of familiarity with. Moreover, the operation of the court system has two core streams of activity, the administration of the courts and legal decision-making. As you read the chapter, keep asking yourself about the parallels between the use of AI in the courts and the use of AI in your organization.

Important Note: The analysis in this chapter is hypothetical. It is not based on an actual court system. Rather, it illustrates how to think through the application of the AI use case identification and prioritization framework in a real-world environment.

Learning Questions and Food for Thought

1. What insights can you take from this example that will inform how you adopt AI in your organization?

While we showed you in the previous chapter a real-life example with the hungry judges and bail hearings, this chapter shows how one could apply the framework we just outlined to the administration of the judicial court system. This content is only illustrative, not based on a specific judicial system. We intend for the materials to provide a general template and thought-starters for how to apply the framework in your own specific context, but we provide citations when using factual information.

The core process stages of the court system are fourfold: pleadings, discovery, trial, and judgment. Completing this process involves administrative tasks and substantive decisions. We apply the AI use case framework below.

Profile and Assess Core Functions

The starting point for identifying and prioritizing AI use cases in the court system is detailing the core functions performed. From the administrative perspective, managing the workforce, court facilities, and physical evidence, documents, and digital content are core. We detail the key functions in Figure 10.1.

The substantive tasks often involve legal research and analysis. Decision-making is the primary substantive responsibility of the courts and covers a broad spectrum of activities, the most important of which are setting bail, determining fault, and determining sanctions; sentencing in criminal cases; and compensation/restitution in civil matters (see Figure 10.2).

The assessment criteria for the core functions are quality, efficiency, and equity. From an administrative viewpoint, quality is a clear, predictable, and reliable process. The agency achieves efficiency when all resources, people, facilities, equipment/technology are used with minimal waste. Equity refers to equal treatment of all participants in the process regardless of race, socioeconomic status, location, gender, language, and so on. Using red, yellow, and green as an assessment grade for "poor," "all right," and "good," the following is the evaluation of the administrative core functions in our hypothetical court system:

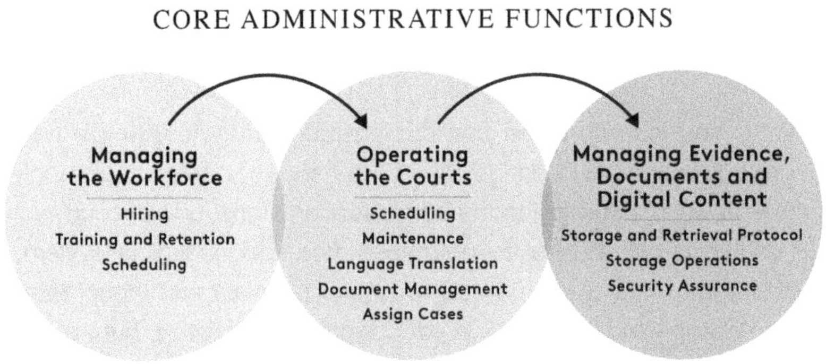

CORE ADMINISTRATIVE FUNCTIONS

Figure 10.1 Core administrative functions. Generated by the authors.

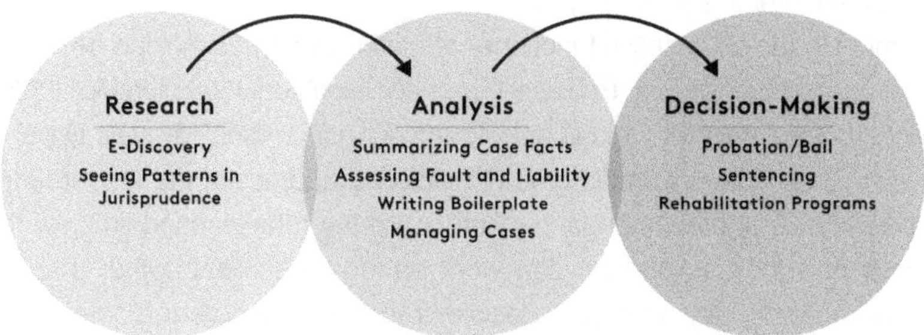

Figure 10.2 Core substantiative functions. Generated by the authors.

- Managing the workforce: Red

  - Quality: unpredictable schedules, poor retention (20 percent annual turnover versus 12 percent in other government agencies).

  - Efficiency: recruitment process takes three weeks longer than benchmark.

  - Equity: failing to meet diversity objectives.

- Managing the court facilities: Red

  - Quality: facilities need $25 million to be in a state of good repair, frequent HVAC problems, spotty internet.

  - Efficiency: maintenance costs 15 percent above industry standard; utilization of courtrooms is only 55 percent, 15 percent below industry standards.

  - Equity: unreliable translation services cause delays and associated costs; courts in lower socioeconomic locations are in a worse physical condition.

- Managing documents and digital content: Red

  - Quality: document files are well organized and easily accessed, but limited use of digital archival technology.

  - Efficiency: accelerated use of digital storage offers $1.5 million in document retention budget.

  - Equity: all courts have access to the same document management process and technology.

The bottom line is that there is a significant opportunity for improvement in the administration of this judicial system.

Turning to the substantive functions, we define quality as making decisions based on comprehensive, unbiased, and apolitical legal scholarship. It also reflects the accuracy of judicial decision-making. For example, was Driver A or Driver B at fault in a traffic crash? Efficiency addresses the time it takes to complete legal proceedings. Indicators are the total elapsed time for the process and the time judges can work on legal decisions rather than on administration. Equity considers decisions that are consistent regardless of race, gender, socioeconomic status, or age, and where judicial biases are minimized.

The assessment reveals the research and analysis activities are yellow and decision-making is green. We have provided details and the supporting rationale below.

- Research and analysis: Yellow

  - Quality: several decisions were overturned based on weak research/analysis scholarship.

  - Efficiency: information is readily and easily accessible to all parties at the court and remotely.

  - Equity: few decisions are overturned based on bias/discrimination.

- Decision-making: Green

  - Quality: few decisions are appealed, fewer are overturned.

  - Efficiency: court backlog and total elapsed time are less than benchmarks; judges spend less than 15 percent of their time on administration compared to the 20 percent benchmark.

  - Equity: academic study of court decisions reveals minimal instances of bias in decision-making.

Figure 10.3 provides a summary of the assessments. These assessments are the inputs to segmentation and prioritization, the next step.

Segment and Prioritize the "Reds"

The potential applications of AI in most organizations are expansive, yet the capacity for adoption is limited. Therefore, prioritization is key. The functions

ASSESSMENT OF KEY FUNCTIONS

ADMINISTRATIVE FUNCTIONS

Managing the Workforce ⭐

Operating the Courts ⭐

Managing Evidence/
Documents/Digital Content ⭐

SUBSTANTIVE FUNCTIONS

Research ⭐ ⭐

Analysis ⭐ ⭐

Decision-Making ⭐ ⭐ ⭐

Figure 10.3 Assessment of key functions. Generated by the authors.

CRITICALITY MAPPING OF THE TASK-LEVEL "REDS"

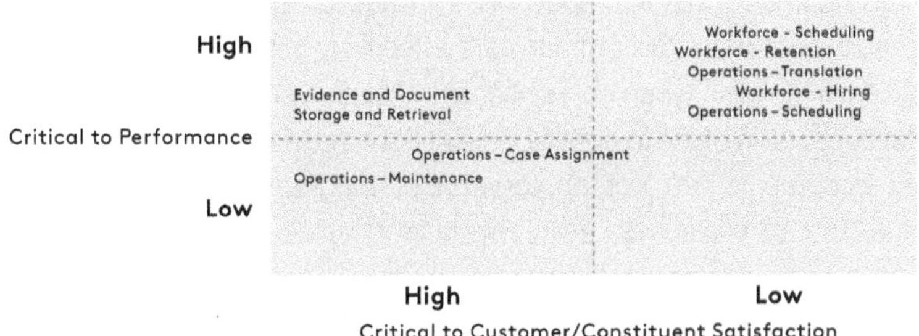

Figure 10.4 Criticality mapping of the task-level "reds". Generated by the authors.

profiled in Step 1 provide the reds, those activities where there is significant opportunity for improvement. In this illustration, these include managing the workforce, court facilities, and evidence/document/digital content. These broad categories should be unpacked to specific activities, as AI applications are generally task-specific. For example, we can unpack the need for better management of the workforce into hiring, training and retention, and scheduling.

The AI priorities emerge by considering the criticality of each specific task: critical to performance and critical to customers/constituents. Figure 10.4 shows the criticality mapping. Managing several aspects of the workforce, translation services, and scheduling courtrooms are top priorities.

Identify AI Applications for Top-priority Reds

The critical reds are the most pressing areas for improvement in the court system. Adopting AI is predicated on the availability of AI applications. As mentioned above, being a fast follower (using existing AI applications) is preferable to being on the leading (or often "bleeding") edge.

In this illustrative example, the one priority is providing translation services. The court system guarantees litigants, attorneys, and witnesses real-time translation to their native language for both oral and text communications. Routinely, translators are not available, leading to delays in proceedings that are costly for the court and its "customers." The root causes of this failure are (1) a lack of translators, especially in minority areas; (2) a lack of translators in less widely used languages; (3) low compensation levels and no payment for travel time and cost; and (4) a lack of sufficient lead time to arrange for services.

AI is routinely being used for translation in business and government. For example, US Customs and Border Protection developed CBP Translate to enable its agents to communicate effectively with travelers who are not proficient in English when conventional translation services are not available. Protections are in place to obtain consent from the traveler to use the program; travel documents are not photographed; biographical information is not captured for US citizens or Lawful Permanent Residents; and the conversation history is deleted after ninety days.[1]

Another example is the use of an AI translation chatbot by the Minnesota Department of Public Safety's Driver and Vehicle Services. The AI program provides translation in multiple languages including Spanish and Somali. The system provides interactive information such as updating insurance and updates in title and license status. The project was initiated as a result of customer input that indicated the language barrier was a major challenge for many in the state. The chatbot is powered by Google AI.[2]

In legal settings, however, the use of AI translation is still under consideration. Given the importance of addressing the court translation problem and that few options exist, assessing AI translation is justified. Of course, the return on investment needs to be high to overcome the leading-edge risk.

This same process is completed for each of the red functions.

Assess AI Solutions

Knowing that AI translation is used in government settings, the next task is determining if AI is a viable solution in the court context and, indeed, is the best solution. AI may be the best solution if it meets the following conditions:

- AI providers have the capacity to design, implement and support your solution.

- Your organization has the expertise to use the AI application and management is prepared to support the change management process.

If these conditions are met, the next question is: Does using AI generate not only a positive return on investment but also a superior return compared to the non-AI alternatives? The return on investment is estimated based on the costs and benefits of the AI application. Figure 10.5 provides an illustrative example of the key factors for consideration.

The costs include:

- Initial development or use fee;

- Ongoing operating/computing and maintenance;

- Implementation, change management, and training;

- Quality control;

- Privacy and security functions.

Some of these are cash outlays for hardware, software, and expertise; others are using employee time and other organizational resources. The costs are

COST AND BENEFIT FACTORS

Cost Factors

Direct
- Development or Use Fees
- Operating/Computing and Maintenance
- Quality Control and Security

Indirect
- Change Management and Training

Benefit Factors

Direct
- Faster Proceedings
- Labor Savings

Indirect
- More Accurate and Equitable Outcomes
- Uniform Translations

Risk Considerations
- Cost: Underestimate Cost and Time for Implementation
- Benefit: Overestimate Improvement in Justice and Savings

Figure 10.5 Cost and benefit factors. Generated by the authors.

readily expressed in dollars. Of note, the cost of computing can be substantial. There is a trade-off between more comprehensive models, but these have higher computing costs. Narrower models are likely to be more feasible for courts where budgets are constrained.

The benefits are internal efficiencies and external customer satisfaction. Internal efficiencies could include a reduction in translation costs as AI substitutes for labor. The availability of AI translation at scale could also speed up court proceedings, improving the utilization of juridical resources. Moreover, AI is likely to enhance consistency through uniform translations. The labor reduction benefits can be directly converted into dollar savings, and we can also estimate resource efficiencies. For example, if proceedings delays caused by waiting for translators are reduced by ten minutes per day and there are six staff members impacted, there are an hour per day of labor savings. The value of this is the average labor cost per hour multiplied by the days per year the court operates.

The external customer benefits have both tangible and intangible dimensions. Tangible benefits center on faster proceedings. Less time waiting for translators is valued at an average wage rate. Likely of greater value is a better understanding of the proceedings for the foreign-language speaker and the other participants in the proceeding, which should lead to a more accurate and equitable outcome.

Valuing the customer benefits in general and the right outcome in particular is very difficult. One way to complete the cost-benefit analysis despite this challenge is conducting a breakeven analysis. Compare the costs with the directly quantified benefits. The difference represents the value that the indirect benefits must account for. If the number is small, it is likely the return on investment is positive.

Implementation of any new technology, including AI, has risks. The risks are on the cost side—higher than planned expenses and longer than anticipated implementation. There are also risks that the anticipated benefits will not materialize. Therefore, use conservative estimates and proceed only if the return is strongly positive.

A strong positive return on AI is necessary but not sufficient. The final requirement is that the return is higher than the return on non-AI alternatives. In the foregoing scenario, there were no other alternatives.

The bottom line in this example: if AI translation offers a strong positive return on investment, it should be on the list of AI applications for prioritization.

AI PRIORITY MAPPING

NEAR-TERM PLAN
(next 24 months)

Administrative Functions
1. Workforce – Scheduling
2. Workforce – Retention
3. Operations – Translation
4. Workforce – Hiring

LONG-TERM PLAN
(beyond 24 months)

Administrative Functions
1. Operations – Scheduling
2. Evidence and Document Storage and Retrieval

Substantive Functions
1. Research and Information Summary
2. Assessing Fault and Liability

Figure 10.6 AI priority mapping. Generated by the authors.

Prioritize and Pilot AI Solutions

The fifth and sixth steps in the AI use case prioritization process are developing an overall AI roadmap and pilot-testing the easiest projects first. We recommend two time frames: near-term (one to two years) and long-term (three to five years). The near-term list of AI initiatives should focus on the current reds, where existing AI applications are ideally in use in the courts, but if not, at least in government. Use the "crawl-walk-run" approach to sequencing the projects. Do the easiest first as pilots to build internal capacity and minimize risk. Here, the goal is to understand how best to bring AI into your organization. This also enables your organization to establish a track record of success and value creation, which will fuel subsequent initiatives. View the first few efforts as pilots, where learning is as important as generating the intended return on investment.

The long-term mapping reflects how the initiatives support the organization's overarching strategy. Rather than addressing individual red functions, the long-term plan is directly aligned with mission and vision. A sample map for using AI in the courts is provided in Figure 10.6. Given the pace of innovation in the AI space, the long-term plan informs the indicative direction of the organization's adoption of AI but should be revisited on a semiannual basis to incorporate internal progress on AI use and new external applications being developed.

> What insights can you take from this example that will inform how you adopt AI in your organization?
>
> ____
> ____
> ____

Chapter 11

Beginning with Generative AI

Chapter Summary

Public sector agencies seeking to incorporate artificial intelligence into their operations often find generative AI to be an ideal starting point. These tools—capable of producing text, images, translations, and summaries—are readily accessible, require minimal technical expertise, and integrate easily into existing workflows. By starting with common tasks such as drafting reports, summarizing feedback, or translating content, governments can begin building internal familiarity with AI while delivering immediate benefits in efficiency and service delivery. This "crawl, walk, run" approach allows organizations to begin with off-the-shelf tools and progress toward more tailored solutions as capacity grows.

Around the world, governments are already seeing results. Translation tools like DeepL and LILT are helping agencies in Switzerland and the United States accelerate multilingual communication, while municipalities in China and Canada are embedding generative AI into citizen service platforms and permitting systems. Advanced examples, such as the US Department of Homeland Security's internal AI assistant, demonstrate how agencies can evolve toward secure, customized platforms to support complex tasks. Responsible deployment requires clear governance, strong privacy protections, and ongoing evaluation of efficiency, accuracy, and user adoption. When thoughtfully implemented, generative AI can improve service quality, reduce administrative burden, and strengthen the relationship between governments and the people they serve.

> ## Learning Questions and Food for Thought
>
> 1. What advantages and disadvantages do "off-the-shelf" tools offer for public sector agencies compared to more customized or in-house AI solutions?
> 2. Can you think of a short list of processes or services in your organization where you might want to explore the benefits of generative AI?
> 3. When evaluating generative AI tools, why is it important to assess factors like data privacy, model transparency, and human oversight? How might your agency ensure responsible use of AI while still embracing innovation?

If you are anything like Ben, when you were thirteen years old and hungry, you would head to the freezer and pull out a Pizza Pocket. Was there a wealth of choice in toppings? Not really—you could choose pepperoni, pepperoni-bacon, or four cheese. Were they healthy? Absolutely not. But for someone with no skill in the kitchen, Pizza Pockets were a quick and easy option that outsourced most of the cooking process (save for a few pushes of a microwave button) to a food company to provide a reliable, filling meal. By college, however, Ben started to become a bit more adventurous in the kitchen, using pizza kits to get his Italian food fix. These kits required more effort but also allowed for more customization—the dough needed to be mixed and kneaded, the can of sauce needed to be spread, but he could customize his toppings based on his preferences and add as much cheese as he wanted.

By the time Ben was in the working world, he had become a bit of a pizza aficionado. He owned a pizza stone and other tools to help improve the quality and taste of his finished product, and was making dough and sauce from scratch and experimenting with a range of more creative toppings like hot honey, feta cheese, pesto, and arugula.

Ben's progression from Pizza Pockets to pizza-making proficiency illustrates the "crawl, walk, run" approach that we advocate in this book for adopting AI in your organization. First, you find an AI application that you can purchase off the shelf. This gives you the opportunity to get a sense of what is useful and where you would like to grow your efforts in the future but will not allow for much customization (or any at all). With this first foray into the AI world under your belt, you will be able to speak with more fluency in this space, determining what is lacking with your current capabilities, working with your own internal team and outside experts on a more optimized service with features that offer your team and your constituents better value. From here, you will be able to evaluate and evolve, ultimately leading to the ability to "run." You'll be able to build sufficient in-house expertise to implement a bespoke solution that meets all your expectations and, when it comes up short, you'll have the ability to make necessary changes.

To start you on your journey, we encourage you to consider generative AI as the first step. In the rest of this chapter, we offer a refresher on what generative AI is and why we believe it is a valuable stepping stone for a government agency dipping its toe into the AI pool. Then we offer a few examples of public agencies in the crawl, walk, and run stages of generative AI use and finish the chapter with the next steps to take as you look for a generative AI use case that you can use for your initial project.

Generative AI: A Quick Refresher

As we discussed in Part I, generative AI refers to a class of artificial intelligence models designed to create new content—such as text, images, audio, video, or even computer code—that closely resembles what a human might produce. Unlike traditional AI systems that classify data or make predictions based on existing inputs, generative AI learns patterns, structures, and styles from vast datasets and uses that knowledge to generate entirely new outputs. These models, like GPT (text generation) or DALL-E (image generation), are often based on advanced architectures such as transformers and use deep learning techniques to recognize intricate relationships within the data they are trained on. Essentially, generative AI works by predicting what comes next—whether that's the next word in a sentence or the next pixel in an image—and refining its outputs through a process of continual feedback and optimization.

For government agencies and employees, generative AI offers powerful tools to improve efficiency, accessibility, and service delivery. It can assist with drafting policy documents, preparing reports, summarizing large volumes of public feedback, or translating information into plain language for diverse audiences. Agencies can use it to generate public service announcements, automate routine correspondence, enhance citizen engagement through personalized communications, or support research and analysis efforts. By automating time-consuming tasks and providing high-quality drafts that staff can quickly review and finalize, generative AI helps government employees focus more on critical thinking, decision-making, and public service, ultimately improving responsiveness, transparency, and the citizen experience.

Generative AI: A Good Place to Start

For public servants exploring how to begin using artificial intelligence in general, generative AI can provide an ideal entry point. Unlike highly specialized AI systems that require major data engineering, technical infrastructure, or deep customization, many generative AI tools are already accessible, flexible, pre-trained, and easy to integrate into existing workflows. You will not need to gather data to feed into a model to help the system learn. Using generative AI, departments can quickly test applications like drafting reports, summarizing public consultation feedback, generating outreach materials, or improving internal communications—all without needing a large upfront investment. Starting with generative AI also offers a low-risk way to build internal familiarity with AI capabilities, governance needs, and responsible use practices, while directly supporting goals like efficiency, transparency, and citizen engagement.

Several companies offer generative AI tools that you can experiment with depending on your needs; some of these tools might even be integrated into software you are already using. For text-based tasks, platforms like OpenAI's ChatGPT Enterprise, Anthropic's Claude, and Google's Gemini provide secure and customizable options. For document drafting and editing, tools like Microsoft Copilot (already integrated into Word and Outlook platforms) and Google Duet AI (within Google Workspace) allow public servants to apply AI inside familiar software environments. For image generation and communications design, services like Adobe Firefly offer AI-powered creativity with enterprise-grade controls. Importantly, many of these providers now offer "enterprise" or "government" versions, with enhanced privacy, security, and model transparency—helping departments ensure compliance with data governance and ethical standards.

> What advantages and disadvantages do "off-the-shelf" tools offer for public sector agencies compared to more customized or in-house AI solutions?

Given that some of these AI products come with your monthly software subscription, a logical place to start might be simply exploring your existing tools to ensure you are taking full advantage of the ways in which AI can optimize and improve your workflow. To give you a sense of the progression of AI use cases, we offer examples below of government agencies that are in the "crawl," "walk," and "run" stages of generative AI use.

Crawling, Walking, and Running with Generative AI

Most government agencies that have adopted generative AI are in the "crawl" or "walk" stages of development, with many reporting promising results even from the simple adoption of "off-the-shelf" products. A popular first tool for agencies trying generative AI is translation software. The Swiss government, for instance, uses DeepL translation to translate official documents into English, French, and Italian, cutting a job that takes a human days to complete down to mere minutes.[1] For the last four years, the US National Weather Service and National Hurricane Center have similarly contracted with LILT, a translation platform, to provide weather updates in Spanish, Chinese, Vietnamese, and Samoan. This partnership has cut the amount of time it takes to issue translations to the public from one hour to less than ten minutes.[2] Schools, like Chinook Middle School in Bellevue, Washington, are also purchasing and deploying Microsoft's Translator for PowerPoint and the Microsoft Translator app at events like parent-teacher meetings to enable all parents and teachers to easily understand the conversation and ask and listen to replies to questions in their preferred language.[3]

When using AI translation applications, remember that generative AI is far from perfect. Humans need to verify the quality of the translation. Also, there are some applications where the risk is low (e.g., promoting local community activities) and high (e.g., translating legal documents). Start with low-risk applications to learn and then progress to higher-risk uses.

Meanwhile, examples abound in China, where municipalities are using DeepSeek to improve service. In the city of Meizhou, officials integrated DeepSeek into the query dashboard its public service hotline operators use. Operators are now able to use AI to not only retrieve information but also craft responses to send to citizens calling or emailing in. Early results show that the tool has made operators more efficient, improving response speed and resolution times by 25–30 percent.[4]

Starting to walk, the IT team of the city of Kelowna, British Columbia has codeveloped two generative AI tools, one using Zammo.ai to answer constituents' questions on permitting and the second using Copilot software to guide developers through the municipal development application process.[5] Collaborating with the planning team, the IT team worked to understand the needs and common questions citizens had about permitting, then ran Agile sprints to develop solutions and gather feedback from the planners and external property developers.[6] They worked with Microsoft's AI team to learn the possible applications of AI, and the benefits and drawbacks, and the planners and developers guided the IT team on how the chatbot needed to work to be useful. Though this project is only just getting underway in public application, the IT team intends to compare how long application tasks used to take when done manually as compared to how long they take with AI automation, and measure the volume of questions answered by the chatbot service.[7]

As generative AI use is still in its infancy in the public sector, some of the most advanced applications are in the defense space. The US Department of Homeland Security (DHS) has introduced DHSChat, an internally developed generative AI chatbot designed to assist over 19,000 headquarters employees with tasks such as drafting reports, summarizing information, and developing software. Created by the DHS AI Corps, DHSChat operates within a secure environment and leverages external large language models via API, ensuring that data from the chatbot is not used to train external models. The tool aims to enhance efficiency while maintaining high standards of security and privacy.[8]

The agency has previously allowed employees to experiment with commercial generative AI tools like ChatGPT and Claude for publicly available information. Building on this experience, DHSChat enables staff to perform routine work more efficiently, including summarizing complex documents, generating computer code, and streamlining repetitive tasks like data entry.[9] Looking ahead, DHS plans to evolve DHSChat into a secure internal knowledge hub that employees can query for information about DHS policies, data, and other internal resources.[10]

The Roadmap to Generative AI

If you think generative AI is the right place to begin your agency's AI journey, then you will want to look at challenges where generative AI might be the right tool. The primary areas are for tasks that involve creating or transforming content, especially when that content follows patterns or structures learned from large datasets.

Specifically, it's strongest in the following areas:

1. **Drafting and Content Creation**

   – Writing first drafts of documents, reports, emails, articles, or marketing materials;

   – Summarizing long texts into key points;

   – Expanding short ideas into more detailed content;

   – Translating text into different languages or into plain language.

2. **Data Synthesis and Analysis**

   – Summarizing large amounts of qualitative data (e.g., public comments, feedback surveys);

   – Generating summaries of complex research, news articles, or regulations;

   – Drafting briefing notes or reports from multiple sources.

3. **Personalization and Communication**

   – Creating tailored messages for different audiences (e.g., emails, public notices, FAQs);

   – Chatbots that can answer routine questions based on learned patterns;

   – Personalized recommendations or information retrieval.

4. **Idea Generation and Brainstorming**

   – Helping users brainstorm new ideas (e.g., program names, policy options, public engagement strategies);

   – Generating lists of possible solutions to a given problem;

   – Drafting early versions of creative content like slogans, visual concepts, or scenarios.

5. **Design and Visual Creation**

   – Generating draft images, graphics, and visual layouts (e.g., Adobe Firefly, DALL-E);

  - Assisting with creative projects like slide decks, posters, and social media graphics;

6. Automation of Routine Tasks

  - Automating the creation of meeting summaries, case notes, or service tickets;

  - Assisting in creating templates or forms;

  - Helping code simple scripts or basic web pages.

In all these applications, generative AI works best when used as a helper, not a replacement. It is excellent for first drafts, ideas, and bulk work—but human review is still critical for accuracy, tone, nuance, legality, and ethics, especially in government and sensitive sectors.

> Can you think of a short list of processes or services in your organization where you might want to explore the benefits of generative AI?
>
> ____
> ____
> ____
> ____

Factors to Consider

When assessing generative AI tools for your government use, data privacy and security compliance should be a primary focus. You will need to ensure the tool meets recognized government security standards such as FedRAMP, SOC 2, or ISO 27001. Just as important is model transparency and explainability; you will want to purchase tools where providers can offer clear documentation about how their model was trained, including details about training datasets and any efforts to mitigate bias. You should also verify whether you have the ability to audit or inspect model outputs to maintain accountability.

Customization and integration capabilities are critical to ensure the tool fits your agency's unique needs. You can assess how easily the tool can be tailored through prompts, fine-tuning, or specific settings, and how much control you retain over any outputs. Additionally, the tool's usability plays a major role in adoption; it should integrate smoothly into existing software environments such as Microsoft Office or government CRM systems and be accessible for your nontechnical staff. Accuracy and relevance of outputs are also key—especially in specialized fields like legal, healthcare, or regulatory environments—where even small errors could have significant consequences.

Finally, operational considerations such as cost, scalability, ethics, and vendor reliability should not be overlooked. Your team must evaluate whether the pricing model is sustainable for both pilot projects and eventual broader deployment, and whether the tool can handle increasing workloads without performance issues. Ethical safeguards—such as hallucination detection, misinformation filtering, and human oversight mechanisms—are essential to responsible AI use. Lastly, the long-term stability of the vendor and the availability of high-quality, government-focused customer support are important to ensure continuity and minimize operational risks over time.

To that end, some of the key questions to ask vendors include the following:

Data and Privacy

- Where is data processed and stored? Is data shared with third parties?
- Can the model operate in a "zero data retention" mode?

Model Training and Bias

- What datasets were used to train the model?
- What steps have been taken to mitigate bias or prevent harmful outputs?

Control and Governance

- Can we restrict the model's behavior with agency-specific rules (e.g., compliance language, tone)?
- Are there features for monitoring, logging, and auditing AI interactions?

Performance and Limits

- What is the model's known error rate or hallucination rate?
- Are there character/word/usage limits per query or per month?

Security and Accreditation

- Does the tool have certifications relevant to public sector use?
- Has it undergone external security audits or penetration testing?

Adaptability and Future-Proofing

- How often is the model updated, and are there risks with updates impacting performance?

- Can we easily retrain or switch models if needed?

Cost and Contractual Flexibility

- Is there a government-specific licensing model?

- Are there flexible options for pilots, scaling up, or exiting if needed?

When deploying generative AI tools, your staff should define clear metrics for success to ensure the technology is meeting both operational and ethical goals. One key metric is efficiency gains, such as reductions in time spent on drafting documents, synthesizing data, or answering routine inquiries. Output quality should also be tracked, measuring the factual accuracy, relevance, and readability of AI-generated content. User adoption rates—including how many employees are using the tool regularly and whether it integrates seamlessly into daily workflows—provide valuable insight into usability and value. Additionally, error rates or hallucination detection rates can help agencies monitor and mitigate potential risks over time.

Beyond operational performance, you should also assess public trust and compliance metrics. This can include tracking how well outputs align with ethical guidelines, accessibility standards, and security/privacy regulations. Feedback loops are important, both from internal users and from any members of the public interacting with AI-assisted services. You may also want to measure return on investment (ROI), not just in financial terms but also through qualitative impacts like improved citizen engagement, faster service delivery, or enhanced staff satisfaction. Together, these metrics ensure that any generative AI deployments you undertake are not only efficient but also responsible, sustainable, and aligned with a broader public service mission.

When evaluating generative AI tools, why is it important to assess factors like data privacy, model transparency, and human oversight? How might your agency ensure responsible use of AI while still embracing innovation?

____

____

____

____

Conclusion

We appreciate the time investment you have made in reading the book. We trust the content will help you further your understanding of AI and how it can be prudently adopted in your organization. Four suggestions as you move forward:

1. Context matters. Use the information in the book but adjust the substance to meet your organization's unique circumstances.

2. Crawl to walk to run. Adopting AI is like training for a marathon. Start slowly and build up your experience and expertise. The risks are real, so mitigate them.

3. The benefits can be a game-changer for your team, so put your toe in the water.

4. If you have questions, Mark and Ben are happy to share their expertise with you and help you tap the full potential of AI today and tomorrow.

Appendix A
Sample AI Ethics Policy

1. Purpose

This policy establishes requirements for transparency in AI systems used by (Government Agency) to ensure accountability, public trust, and fair decision-making.

2. Scope

This policy applies to all AI-driven processes, decision-making tools, and automated systems used by (Government Agency) in public services, policymaking, and regulatory functions.

3. Core Principles

3.1 Explainability

- AI systems must be designed to allow government employees, affected individuals, and oversight bodies to understand how decisions are made.

- All AI models must have accompanying documentation explaining their logic, data sources, and limitations in nontechnical language.

- AI-generated decisions that significantly impact individuals must include a plain-language explanation of how the decision was reached.

3.2 Public Disclosure

- A publicly accessible AI Use Register will document all AI systems used by the agency, including:

  - Purpose of the AI system;

  - Data sources and types used;

  - General functioning and decision-making logic;

  - Risk assessment, including potential biases and mitigation strategies;

  - Third-party vendors involved, if any.

- This register will be updated at least every six months.

3.3 Data Transparency

- AI systems must disclose what data they rely on, including the source, collection methods, and whether personal data is used.

- If personal data is processed, individuals must be informed of:

    - How their data is being used;

    - Their rights to request, review, and correct AI-influenced decisions;

    - Opt-out options when applicable.

3.4 Notification of AI Use

- Stakeholders must be informed whenever they are interacting with an AI system.

- If an AI system has played a role in a decision that impacts an individual (e.g., job hiring, loan approval, law enforcement action, government benefits), the affected party must be explicitly notified of AI involvement and provided with an explanation of how AI influenced the decision.

- Notifications must be clear, timely, and accessible, ensuring individuals understand their rights regarding AI-influenced decisions.

3.5 Algorithmic Impact Assessments (AIAs)

- Before deploying an AI system, an Algorithmic Impact Assessment (AIA) must be conducted, covering:

    - Potential biases in training data and model performance;

    - Risks of discrimination or unfair treatment;

    - Steps taken to mitigate risks;

    - Review mechanisms for ensuring accuracy and fairness.

- AIAs will be publicly available for systems affecting public services.

3.6 Human Oversight

- AI-driven decisions that affect legal rights, employment, housing, or healthcare must have a human-in-the-loop review process before final action.

- AI decisions that trigger adverse outcomes for individuals will require a secondary review by a human official.

3.7 Redress and Appeals

- Individuals must have a clear and accessible way to challenge AI-influenced decisions.
- A dedicated AI Ombudsman or oversight committee will handle AI-related grievances and ensure timely responses.

3.8 External Audits

- Independent third-party audits will be conducted annually to ensure AI systems comply with transparency and fairness standards.
- Audit findings will be publicly released.

4. Compliance and Accountability

- Violations of this policy will result in corrective actions, including system review, retraining of AI models, or removal of the AI system.
- A designated Chief AI Ethics Officer will oversee compliance and enforcement.

5. Implementation and Review

- This policy will be reviewed and updated annually to reflect technological advancements, legal changes, and public feedback.

Appendix B
Sample Key Contract Language When Sharing Data for AI Use

1. Data Protection Obligations

- The Service Provider shall implement and maintain reasonable administrative, physical, and technical safeguards to protect confidential information and personal data from unauthorized access, use, disclosure, alteration, or destruction.
- The Service Provider agrees to use industry-standard encryption for data at rest and in transit when handling confidential information.
- The Service Provider shall limit access to confidential information to only those employees, subcontractors, or agents who require access to perform services under this Agreement.

2. Compliance with Laws and Standards

- The Service Provider shall comply with all applicable US federal, state, and local laws governing data security, privacy, and cybersecurity.
- The Service Provider shall ensure that any third parties, subcontractors, or affiliates comply with the same security and privacy standards as outlined in this Agreement.

3. Data Access and Confidentiality

- The Service Provider shall ensure that all personnel with access to government data undergo appropriate background checks, security clearances, and training on handling controlled information, classified data, or sensitive government records.
- The Service Provider shall implement role-based access controls and multi-factor authentication to restrict access to confidential information.

- The Service Provider shall maintain an audit log of all access to confidential information and provide such records to the Client upon request.

- The Service Provider shall not use confidential information for any purpose other than providing the services agreed upon in this Agreement.

4. Incident Response and Data Breach Notification

- The Service Provider shall maintain and follow a written Incident Response Plan in the event of a suspected or actual data breach, cybersecurity incident, or unauthorized access.

- The Service Provider shall notify the Client in writing within (X) hours/days of becoming aware of a data breach, providing:

  - A summary of the incident, including the scope of data affected.
  - Steps taken to mitigate the breach.
  - Any required reporting obligations under applicable law.

- The Service Provider shall cooperate fully with the Client's investigation, remediation, and notification process related to the breach.

5. Data Retention, Deletion, and Ownership

- The Service Provider shall retain data only for as long as necessary to perform services under this Agreement.

- Upon termination or expiration of this Agreement, or upon the Client's written request, the Service Provider shall securely delete or return all confidential information, including backups, in compliance with industry standards.

- The Client retains all ownership rights over data, records, and information processed by the Service Provider. Upon contract termination or upon written request, the Service Provider shall securely delete or return all government data.

6. Audit Rights and Security Assessments

- The Client reserves the right to conduct or request security audits, penetration testing, compliance reviews, or system vulnerability assessments of the Service Provider's data security practices at any time.

- The Service Provider shall promptly remediate any identified vulnerabilities and provide the Client with a written plan of action upon request.

7. Liability and Indemnification

- The Service Provider shall be liable for any unauthorized access, breach, or data compromise caused by its negligence, willful misconduct, or failure to comply with this Agreement.

- The Service Provider shall indemnify and hold harmless the Client from any claims, damages, fines, or penalties arising from a breach of data security caused by the Service Provider's noncompliance.

Appendix C
Sample Contract Language for AI Contractors and Service Providers

1. Data Backup Requirements

- The Service Provider shall implement and maintain a comprehensive backup strategy to ensure the integrity and availability of all Client data processed, stored, or transmitted by the AI system.

- Backups shall be performed at least (frequency, e.g., daily, hourly), with retention periods of (X) days/weeks/months unless otherwise agreed upon in writing.

- The Service Provider shall maintain redundant copies of backups across geographically diverse data centers to ensure resilience against data loss.

2. Backup Security and Compliance

- All backup data shall be encrypted using industry-standard encryption protocols both at rest and in transit.

- The Service Provider shall ensure that backup storage locations comply with applicable data privacy and security regulations and other relevant legal requirements.

- Access to backup files shall be restricted to authorized personnel only and shall be protected using multi-factor authentication.

3. Data Restoration and Disaster Recovery

- In the event of data corruption, accidental deletion, or system failure, the Service Provider shall ensure full data restoration within (X) hours from the latest available backup.

- The Service Provider shall maintain a Disaster Recovery Plan that outlines the procedures and timelines for backup restoration following a cybersecurity incident, natural disaster, or system outage.

- The Client shall have the right to request a data restoration test every (X) months to validate backup integrity and recovery processes.

4. Client Access to Backups

- The Client shall have on-demand access to backup data upon request, subject to security authentication measures.

- In case of contract termination, the Service Provider shall provide the Client with a complete backup of all relevant data in a machine-readable format within (X) days of termination, and shall securely delete all copies thereafter unless legally required to retain them.

5. Reporting and Auditing

- The Service Provider shall maintain detailed backup logs and provide periodic reports to the Client, including:

  - Date and time of last successful backup.

  - Retention status and integrity verification results.

  - Any failed backup attempts and corrective actions taken.

- The Client reserves the right to conduct audits of backup procedures and security measures upon reasonable notice.

Appendix D
Self-Assessment

We suspect as you were reading in Chapter 7 about the expertise required for adopting AI, you were informally assessing your organization's position vis-a-vis the requirements. In this appendix, we provide a more formal structure for completing an assessment of your organization's strengths and gaps. In the following set of assessment questions, we erred on the side of being more comprehensive. There is no need to use all the questions. Only ask those that are relevant for your organization and its AI context.

1. Leadership and Strategy

- Does the organization have a clear vision for integrating AI into public service delivery?

- Are leadership and senior management actively engaged in AI discussions and initiatives?

- Is there a strategic plan that includes AI as a tool for innovation or service improvement?

- Has the organization identified specific goals or KPIs for AI implementation?

- Are leaders prepared to champion AI projects and manage change within the organization?

2. Governance and Policy

- Are there established policies or guidelines for AI use within the organization?

- Does the organization have a framework for ethical AI use (e.g., fairness, transparency, and accountability)?

- How does the organization ensure compliance with data protection regulations (e.g., GDPR, HIPAA, or local data privacy laws)?

- Are there protocols in place to address algorithmic bias or unintended consequences of AI systems?

- Has the organization developed a process for citizen engagement regarding AI-related decisions?

3. Data Readiness

- Does the organization have access to sufficient data for AI use cases?
- Is the data structured, clean, and stored in a centralized system for easy access?
- Are data privacy and security protocols in place to protect sensitive information?
- Are there known data gaps or inconsistencies that could impact AI implementation?

4. Technological Infrastructure

- Does the organization have the necessary hardware and software to support AI tools?
- Are cloud computing services or high-performance computing capabilities available?
- Is the existing IT infrastructure scalable to accommodate future AI deployments?
- Are legacy systems capable of integrating with AI technologies, or will they need to be upgraded?
- Does the organization have a plan for ongoing maintenance and updates of AI systems?

5. Workforce and Skills

- Does the organization have in-house expertise in AI, data science, and related fields?
- Are there training programs in place to upskill employees in AI technologies and applications?
- How familiar are staff with interpreting and using AI outputs for decision-making?
- Is there a plan to recruit or collaborate with external AI experts where in-house expertise is lacking?
- Are change management strategies in place to help employees adapt to AI adoption?

6. Budget and Resource Allocation

- Is there a dedicated budget for AI-related initiatives and projects?
- Has the organization allocated resources for research, development, and deployment of AI?
- Are there financial plans in place to maintain and scale AI solutions once implemented?
- Is the organization exploring grants or partnerships to fund AI initiatives?

7. Risk Management and Monitoring

- Does the organization have a process for assessing risks associated with AI adoption?
- Are there mechanisms to monitor and evaluate the performance of AI systems after deployment?
- How will the organization address unintended consequences or errors in AI systems?
- Is there a feedback loop to continuously improve AI solutions based on outcomes and public input?

8. Ethical and Social Impact

- How will the organization ensure that AI solutions promote equity and avoid discrimination?
- Are there safeguards in place to maintain transparency in AI-driven decisions?
- How will the organization communicate the benefits and limitations of AI to citizens?
- Has the organization considered the societal impact of AI adoption, including job displacement and public trust?

You can use a scoring system to assess your readiness more formally. You might use a 3-point scale where 3 is ready to go, 2 is foundation exists but more development is needed, and 1 signifies a significant gap. While not all eight areas need to be ready to go before beginning your AI journey, leadership and strategy, governance and policy, and data readiness are prerequisites.

Appendix E
Specific Problem-Centered Approach

Steps 1 and 2 of the framework (explored in Chapter 9) are designed to examine the entirety of the organization for AI use cases. However, some organizations may have a specific problem they need to tackle and seek to determine if AI offers a solution. In those cases, an alternative approach that narrows the focus of the investigation to addressing the problem is more efficient. This is accomplished by substituting the following tasks for Steps 1 and 2.

Task 1: Define the Problem and Assess Its Root Cause

Solving a problem begins with a clear articulation of the concern. The Kepner-Tregoe framework is effective in defining the problem. The framework asks the typical questions of what (identify the issue), where (locate the issue), when (timing of the concern and when it first appeared), and the magnitude of the issue. Importantly, it also asks the questions: When is it not a problem and where does it not appear? The answers offer important insights, enabling more specific problem definition.

A clear and crisp problem definition is necessary but not sufficient. The root cause of the issue must be determined. There are several approaches to getting to the root cause of the problem. An effective and intuitive approach is the Ishikawa or fishbone diagram. The head of the fish is the effect (i.e., the problem) and the bones are the causes. To ensure a comprehensive identification of the causes, ask: What is the role of policies, process, people, and plant/technology? These four dimensions form the core elements of the fish's skeletal structure. The smaller bones are the specific causes. When drawing the diagram, the more important the issue, the thicker the bone.

Task 2: Identify Solution Options

There are often several options for solving a problem. Some might be policy or process related, others involve people. Others require a technology solution including AI. Several tools support the ideation process. One is SCAMPER.

This acronym stands for substitute, combine, adapt, modify, put to another use, eliminate, and reverse. These words provide a checklist to prompt your thinking on different ways the problem could be solved. Another tool is the ideation loop. You start by imagining a solution. Next, you sketch what that solution looks like in reality. Then you create a model or test to see if it works. The idea of looking is that the process is iterative, continually refining and improving the solution.

Once you have a comprehensive list of potential solutions, you can evaluate them to find the most promising approach. Screening through the options is facilitated with a set of evaluation criteria. Efficacy, the direct improvement in the situation, is one key criterion. Others include operational, political, and financial feasibility. The criteria can be weighted to reflect their comparative importance.

The top option or two will become the focus for the AI assessment that begins in Step 3 of the AI use case framework presented in Chapter 9.

Bibliography

AI Use Case Inventory. "The Government Is Using AI to Better Serve the Public," https://ai.gov/ai-use-cases/.

American Customer Satisfaction Index. "Citizen Satisfaction With Federal Government Services Jumps Again, ACSI Data Show," November 14, 2023, https://theacsi.org/news-and-resources/press-releases/2023/11/14/press-release-federal-government-report-2023/.

Anderson, Hope, Iesha Nunes, and John Oltean. "Newly Passed Colorado AI Act Will Impose Obligations on Developers and Deployers of High-risk AI Systems," White & Case, June 20, 2024, https://www.whitecase.com/insight-alert/newly-passed-colorado-ai-act-will-impose-obligations-developers-and-deployers-high.

Andrews, Lori, and Hannah Bucher. "Automating Discrimination: AI Hiring Practices and Gender Inequality," *Cardoz Law Review* 44, no. 1 (October 2022), https://cardozolawreview.com/automating-discrimination-ai-hiring-practices-and-gender-inequality/.

Antino. "Chatbot Development Cost in 2024," March 3, 2024, https://www.antino.com/blog/chatbot-development-cost.

The Australian. "AI Going to Save Time, Money for Grant Thornton Tax Team," January 5, 2025, https://www.theaustralian.com.au/business/companies/accounting-firms-reveal-how-ai-has-changed-professional-services-and-given-staff-more-time/news-story/12684490bf788397f0dce75817ec64ef.

Blackman, Reid. "Why You Need an AI Ethics Committee," *Harvard Business Review*, July–August 2022, https://hbr.org/2022/07/why-you-need-an-ai-ethics-committee.

Bloomberg Philanthropies. "How Chicago Is Improving Homeless Shelters Through Results-Driven Contracting," 2023, https://whatworkscities.bloomberg.org/cities/chicago-illinois-usa/.

Bohannon, Molly. "Lawyer Used ChatGPT In Court—And Cited Fake Cases. A Judge Is Considering Sanctions," *Forbes*, June 8, 2023, https://www.forbes.com/sites/mollybohannon/2023/06/08/lawyer-used-chatgpt-in-court-and-cited-fake-cases-a-judge-is-considering-sanctions/.

Breaux, Cory, and Emin Dinlersoz. "Only 3.8% of Businesses Use AI to Produce Goods and Services, Highest Use in Information Sector," United States Census Bureau, November 28, 2023, https://www.census.gov/library/stories/2023/11/businesses-use-ai.html.

Brennan Center for Justice. "ICE Extreme Vetting Initiative: A Resource Page,"
    Updated: May 24, 2018. https://www.brennancenter.org/our-work/research-reports
    /ice-extreme-vetting-initiative-resource-page.

Britannica. "Human Intelligence." https://www.britannica.com/science/human
    -intelligence-psychology.

British Columbia News. "New Permitting Strategy Will Help Build Homes Faster,"
    January 16, 2023, https://news.gov.bc.ca/releases/2023WLRS0003-000033.

Broughel, James, and Dustin Chambers. "Learning from State Regulatory
    Streamlining Efforts," National Governors Association, June 2022, 5, https://www
    .nga.org/wp-content/uploads/2022/07/State_Regulation_Report_June2022.pdf.

Care Predict. "Home Care," 2025, https://www.carepredict.com/home-care/.

CBC. "New York State Will Monitor Its Use of AI After Signing New Bill into Law,"
    December 27, 2024, https://www.cbc.ca/news/world/new-york-ai-law-1.7419529.

Chan, Kenneth. "BC Government Unveils New Digital Building Permitting Tool for
    Cities to Use," *Daily Hive*, May 27 2024, https://dailyhive.com/vancouver/bc
    -building-permit-hub-digital-application-tool#.

Christensen, Tom, and Per Lægreid. "The Challenge of Coordination in Central
    Government Organizations: The Norwegian Case," *Public Organization Review*,
    8, no. 2 (2008): 97–116, https://www.researchgate.net/publication/5153878
    _The_Challenge_of_Coordination_in_Central_Government_Organizations_The
    _Norwegian_Case.

City of Chicago, Department of Technology & Innovation, https://www.linkedin.com/
    company/city-of-chicago-dti/about/.

City of San Jose. Government AI Coalition, https://www.sanjoseca.gov/your
    -government/departments-offices/information-technology/ai-reviews-algorithm
    -register/govai-coalition.

City of San Jose. "Information Technology Department Generative AI Guidelines,"
    September 23, 2023, https://www.sanjoseca.gov/your-government/departments
    -offices/information-technology/itd-generative-ai-guideline.

City of Vancouver. "City to Launch Project Requirements Exploration and eComply
    Digital Permitting Tools," June 13, 2023, https://vancouver.ca/news-calendar/city
    -to-launch-project-requirements-exploration-and-ecomply-digital-permitting-tools
    .aspx.

Coffey, Sean. "Long Wait Times Create DMV Headaches; State Officials Say They
    Need More Employees," ABC 11, September 6, 2024, https://abc11.com/post/
    long-wait-times-create-dmv-headaches-state-officials-say-need-more-employees
    /15274897/.

Congressional Budget Office. "Comparing the Compensation of Federal and Private-
    Sector Employees in 2022," April 2024, https://www.cbo.gov/publication/60235.

Corbyn, Zoë. "The Future of Elder Care Is Here—and It's Artificial Intelligence," *The Guardian*, June 3, 2021, https://www.theguardian.com/us-news/2021/jun/03/elder -care-artificial-intelligence-software.

Dastin, Jeffrey. "Amazon Scraps Secret AI Recruiting Tool that Showed Bias Against Women," Reuters, October 10, 2018, https://www.reuters.com/article/world/ insight-amazon-scraps-secret-ai-recruiting-tool-that-showed-bias-against-women -idUSKCN1MK0AG/.

Derick Debevoise, Nell. "The Third Critical Step in Problem Solving that Einstein Missed," *Forbes*, January 26, 2021, https://www.forbes.com/sites/nelldebevoise /2021/01/26/the-third-critical-step-in-problem-solving-that-einstein-missed/.

Duncan, Ian. "Baltimore IT Director Who Was at Helm during Ransomware Attack and City's Recovery Is on Leave," *Baltimore Sun*, September 10, 2019, https:// www.baltimoresun.com/2019/09/10/baltimore-it-director-who-was-at-helm-during -ransomware-attack-and-citys-recovery-is-on-leave/.

Edinger, Julia. "Translation AI Helps Bridge Language Barrier for Minnesota DVS," *Government Technology*, September 28, 2023, https://www.govtech.com/artificial -intelligence/translation-ai-helps-bridge-language-barrier-for-minnesota-dvs.

Eiras Antunes, Miguel. "Surveillance and Predictive Policing Through AI," from *Urban Future with a Purpose*, Deloitte Insights, 2021, https://www.deloitte.com/ an/en/Industries/government-public/perspectives/urban-future-with-a-purpose/ surveillance-and-predictive-policing-through-ai.html.

Ellenberg, Jordan. "Abraham Wald and the Missing Bullet Holes," Medium, July 14, 2016, https://medium.com/@penguinpress/an-excerpt-from-how-not-to-be-wrong -by-jordan-ellenberg-664e708cfc3d.

Ellery, Simon. "Fake Photos of Pope Francis in a Puffer Jacket Go Viral, Highlighting the Power and Peril of AI," CBS News, March 28, 2023, https://www.cbsnews.com/ news/pope-francis-puffer-jacket-fake-photos-deepfake-power-peril-of-ai/.

Fagan, Mark. "AI for the People: The Use of AI to Improve Government Performance," M-RCBG Faculty Working Paper Series 2023-01 (Mossavar-Rahmani Center for Business & Government, Harvard Kennedy School, April 2023), https://www.hks .harvard.edu/centers/mrcbg/publications/fwp/2023-01.

Fagan, Mark. "AI for the People: Use Cases for Government," M-RCBG Faculty Working Paper Series 2024-02 (Mossavar-Rahmani Center for Business & Government, Harvard Kennedy School, August 2024), https://www.hks.harvard .edu/centers/mrcbg/publications/fwp/2024-02.

Federal Trade Commission. "LOCK IT. Protect the Information that You Keep," in *Protecting Personal Information: A Guide for Business*, October 2016, https://www .ftc.gov/business-guidance/resources/protecting-personal-information-guide -business#LockIt.

Federal Trade Commission. "Start with Security: A Guide for Business," August 2023, https://www.ftc.gov/business-guidance/resources/start-security-guide-business.

Fekete, Ágnes. "Data Anonymization Tools: The 4 Best and the 7 Worst Choices for Privacy," Mostly AI, September 28, 2023, https://mostly.ai/blog/data-anonymization -tools.

Fox, Andrea. "AI's Value Is Not Yet Clear in Benefits Administration, Says VA," Healthcare IT News, May 31, 2024, https://www.healthcareitnews.com/news/ais -value-not-yet-clear-benefits-administration-says-va?utm_source=chatgpt.com.

Fox-Sowell, Sophia. "Cyberattacks on State and Local Governments Rose in 2023, Says CIS Report," StateScoop, January 30, 2024, https://statescoop.com/ ransomware-malware-cyberattacks-cis-report-2024/.

García-Herrera Blanco, Cristina. "The Use of Artificial Intelligence by Tax Administrations, A Matter of Principles," *CIAT* (blog), Inter-American Center of Tax Administrations, March 2, 2020, https://www.ciat.org/the-use-of-artificial -intelligence-by-tax-administrations-a-matter-of-principles/?lang=en.

Garvin, David A., and Lynne Levesque. "A Note on Scenario Planning." Harvard Business School Background Note 306-003, November 2005. (Revised July 2006), https://www.hbs.edu/faculty/Pages/item.aspx?num=32841.

Goodman, Ellen P., and Julia Tréhu. "AI Audit-Washing and Accountability," German Marshall Fund of the United States (GMF), November 15, 2022, https://www.gmfus .org/news/ai-audit-washing-and-accountability.

Gordon, Cindy. "2022: The Year of AI Hopes and Horrors," *Forbes*, December 30, 2022, https://www.forbes.com/sites/cindygordon/2022/12/30/ai-hopes-and -horrors/.

GovTribe. "The Veterans Affair (VA) Electronic Health Record Modernization— Integration Office (EHRM-IO) Is in Search for Microsoft Power BI (Power BI) Custom Visualizations," June 2024, https://govtribe.com/opportunity/federal -contract-opportunity/the-veterans-affair-va-electronic-health-record-modernization -integration-office-ehrm-io-is-in-search-for-microsoft-power-bi-power-bi-custom -visualizations-36c10b24q0520.

Hansen, Weslan. "DHS Unveils AI Chatbot for Streamlining Internal Operations," *MeriTalk*, December 18, 2024, https://www.meritalk.com/articles/dhs-unveils-ai -chatbot-for-streamlining-internal-operations/?utm_source=chatgpt.com.

Hattie, John, Dylan Wiliam, and Arran Hamilton. "The Promise and Peril of AI: Will Machines Make Us More or Less Human?" The Educator Australia, August 31, 2023, https://www.theeducatoronline.com/k12/news/the-promise-and-peril-of-ai -will-machines-make-us-more-or-less-human/283150.

Heaven, Will Douglas. "Predictive Policing Algorithms Are Racist. They Need to Be Dismantled," *MIT Technology Review*, July 17, 2020, https://www.technologyreview .com/2020/07/17/1005396/predictive-policing-algorithms-racist-dismantled -machine-learning-bias-criminal-justice/.

Heckman, Jory. "IRS Expands AI-powered Bots to Set Up Payment Plans with Taxpayers over the Phone," Federal News Network, June 17, 2022, https://

federalnewsnetwork.com/artificial-intelligence/2022/06/irs-expands-ai-powered
-bots-to-set-up-payment-plans-with-taxpayers-over-the-phone/.

Heilweil, Rebecca. "ChatGPT, Meet DHSChat: Homeland Security Has a New AI Bot,"
FedScoop, December 17, 2024, https://fedscoop.com/chatgpt-meet-chatdhs
-homeland-security-ai-bot/.

Hendler, James. "As Governments Adopt Artificial Intelligence, There's Little Oversight
and Lots of Danger," Route Fifty, April 19, 2019, https://www.route-fifty.com/digital
-government/2019/04/as-governments-adopt-artificial-intelligence-theres-little
-oversight-and-lots-of-danger/298257/.

Hughes, Abby. "AI Is Helping Outreach Workers in L.A. Predict and Prevent
Homelessness," CBC Radio, October 12, 2023, https://www.cbc.ca/radio
/asithappens/ai-is-helping-outreach-workers-in-l-a-predict-and-prevent
-homelessness-1.6993119.

Hutson, Matthew. "Even Artificial Intelligence Can Acquire Biases Against Race and
Gender," *Science*, April 13, 2017, https://www.science.org/content/article/even
-artificial-intelligence-can-acquire-biases-against-race-and-gender.

International Association of Privacy Professionals (IAPP). US State Privacy Legislation
Tracker, Updated: April 7, 2025, https://iapp.org/resources/article/us-state-privacy
-legislation-tracker/.

ISACA, Artificial Intelligence Fundamentals Certificate, https://www.isaca.org/
credentialing/artificial-intelligence-fundamentals-certificate.

Johnson, Andrew. "The Endless Struggle to Clean Up Rio de Janeiro's Highly Polluted
Guanabara Bay," Mongabay, August 1 2023, https://news.mongabay.com/2023
/08/the-endless-struggle-to-clean-up-rio-de-janeiros-highly-polluted-guanabara
-bay/#:~:text=Five%20centuries%20later%2C%20the%20bay,Planter%20of
%20mangroves.

Kirkpatrick, Keith. "It's Not the Algorithm, It's the Data," *Communications of the
ACM* 60, no. 2 (February 1, 2017): 21–3, https://cacm.acm.org/news/its-not-the
-algorithm-its-the-data/.

Lee, J., et al. "BioBERT: A Pre-trained Biomedical Language Representation Model for
Biomedical Text Mining," *Bioinformatics* 36, no. 4 (February 15, 2020): 1234–40,
https://pmc.ncbi.nlm.nih.gov/articles/PMC7703786/.

Lernende Systeme. "Online Translations at the Touch of a Button," https://www
.plattform-lernende-systeme.de/practical-exampels.html?AID=357&utm_source
=chatgpt.com.

Li, Xinyue, et al. "Bias Behind the Wheel: Fairness Testing of Autonomous Driving
Systems," *ACM Transactions on Software Engineering and Methodology* 1, no. 1
(July 2024), https://arxiv.org/pdf/2308.02935.

Malone, Linda. "Barely Touched by Human Hands: Automation Is Reshaping How
USPS Serves You," *Postal Posts* (blog), United States Postal Service, December

19, 2023, https://uspsblog.com/usps-innovation-in-shipping-automation/#:~:text=Automation%20makes%20this%20work.,we%20call%20flats%20—%20every%20hour.

Massachusetts Executive Office of Technology Services and Security Enterprise Privacy Office. "Enterprise Use and Development of Generative Artificial Intelligence Policy," January 31, 2025, https://www.mass.gov/doc/enterprise-use-and-development-of-generative-artificial-intelligence-policy/download.

Microsoft. "New Study Shows Substantial Potential of Artificial Intelligence for the Swiss Economy," October 3, 2024, https://news.microsoft.com/de-ch/2024/10/03/new-study-shows-substantial-potential-of-artificial-intelligence-for-the-swiss-economy/.

Microsoft. *Transforming Public Sector Services Using Generative AI: Global Case Studies*, Microsoft, February 2024, 6, https://wwps.microsoft.com/wp-content/uploads/2024/02/Transforming-Public-Sector-Services-Generative-AI-Report.pdf.

MindTitan. "AI Use Cases," https://mindtitan.com/resources/industry-use-cases/.

Missouri Leadership Academy, https://leadershipacademy.mo.gov.

MIT Industrial Performance Center. "MIT Work of the Future," https://workofthefuture.mit.edu/research-post/artificial-intelligence-and-the-future-of-work/.

Morrissey, Monique, and Jennifer Sherer. "The Public-sector Pay Gap Is Widening. Unions Help Shrink It," Economic Policy Institute, August 29, 2024, https://www.epi.org/publication/widening-public-sector-pay-gap/#:~:text=Key%20findings,pandemic%20pay%20gap%20of%2013.9%25.

Mulè, Ludovica. "Revolutionizing Waste Management: The Role of AI in Building Sustainable Practices," AI for Good, May 7, 2024, https://aiforgood.itu.int/revolutionizing-waste-management-the-role-of-ai-in-building-sustainable-practices/#:~:text=Lastly%2C%20AI%2Dpowered%20sensors%20integrated,repair%20and%20recycling%20of%20materials.

Narita International Airport Corporation. "Digital Transformation: Automation and Labor Efficiency," https://www.narita-airport.jp/en/company/airport-operation/action/airnarita/automation/.

National Archives. "President Biden Issues Executive Order on Safe, Secure, and Trustworthy Artificial Intelligence," Biden White House, October 30, 2023, https://bidenwhitehouse.archives.gov/briefing-room/statements-releases/2023/10/30/fact-sheet-president-biden-issues-executive-order-on-safe-secure-and-trustworthy-artificial-intelligence/.

National Association of State Chief Information Officers. "State of Ohio—Transforming Delivery of Health & Human Services through Robotics Process Automation," NASCIO Awards, 2019, https://www.nascio.org/wp-content/uploads/2020/09/NASCIO-Awards-2019_State-of-OH-Bots.pdf.

National Conference of State Legislatures. "Artificial Intelligence 2024 Legislation,"
     September 9, 2024, https://www.ncsl.org/technology-and-communication/artificial
     -intelligence-2024-legislation.

New Jersey Office of Innovation. "Impact Report 2024," https://innovation.nj.gov/
     impact-report/2024/about/.

New York & CSEA Partnership. Tuition Benefits Program, https://nyscseapartnership
     .org/tuition-benefits.

New York City. "The New York City Artificial Intelligence Action Plan," October 2023,
     https://www.nyc.gov/assets/oti/downloads/pdf/reports/artificial-intelligence-action
     -plan.pdf.

New York City Council. Law on Automated Employment Decision Tools, 2021, https://
     legistar.council.nyc.gov/LegislationDetail.aspx?ID=4344524&GUID=B051915D
     -A9AC-451E-81F8-6596032FA3F9.

New York City Office of the Mayor. "Mayor Adams Releases First-of-Its-Kind Plan For
     Responsible Artificial Intelligence Use In NYC Government," October 16, 2023,
     https://www.nyc.gov/office-of-the-mayor/news/777-23/mayor-adams-releases-first
     -of-its-kind-plan-responsible-artificial-intelligence-use-nyc#/0.

New York City Office of Technology and Innovation. "OTI Announces Progress on
     Nation's First Comprehensive Artificial Intelligence Action Plan," March 7, 2024,
     https://www.nyc.gov/content/oti/pages/press-releases/oti-announces-progress-on
     -nations-first-comprehensive-artificial-intelligence-action-plan.

New York State. "Governor Hochul Signs Legislative Package to Support New York's
     Hospitality Industry," October 9, 2024, https://www.governor.ny.gov/news/governor
     -hochul-signs-legislative-package-support-new-yorks-hospitality-industry.

News Medical. "AI Revolutionizes Ophthalmology with Oculomics for Cardiovascular
     Risk Assessment," October 4, 2024, https://www.news-medical.net/news
     /20241004/AI-revolutionizes-ophthalmology-with-oculomics-for-cardiovascular-risk
     -assessment.aspx.

Nguyen, Mai-Ann, and Philip McKeown. "5 AI Auditing Frameworks to Encourage
     Accountability," AuditBoard, October 17, 2024, https://www.auditboard.com/blog/
     ai-auditing-frameworks/.

NIH Cloud Lab for AWS. National Institutes for Health STRIDES Initiative, https://cloud
     .nih.gov/resources/cloudlab/aws-jumpstart/?utm_source=chatgpt.com.

O'Brien, Jessie. "How Pinellas County Made Strategic Planning Simple," Polco,
     September 7, 2023, https://blog.polco.us/how-pinellas-county-made-strategic
     -planning-simple.

O'Brien, Matt, and Sarah Parvini. "Trump Signs Executive Order on Developing
     Artificial Intelligence 'Free from Ideological Bias,'" Associated Press, January 23,
     2025, https://apnews.com/article/trump-ai-artificial-intelligence-executive-order-eef
     1e5b9bec861eaf9b36217d547929c.

OECD. Recommendation of the Council on Artificial Intelligence, May 3, 2024, https://
legalinstruments.oecd.org/en/instruments/oecd-legal-0449.

OECD. *Tax Administration 2019: Comparative Information on OECD and Other
Advanced Emerging Economies*. OECD Publishing, 2019, https://read.oecd-ilibrary
.org/taxation/tax-administration-2019_74d162b6-en.

OER Commons. "Intergovernmental Relationships: Unfunded Mandates," https://
oercommons.org/courseware/lesson/15206/student/?section=4.

O'Reilly, Jim. "Choosing a Cloud Provider: 8 Storage Considerations," Network
Computing, September 13, 2017, https://www.networkcomputing.com/cloud
-networking/choosing-a-cloud-provider-8-storage-considerations?utm_source
=chatgpt.com.

Oxford English Dictionary. "Artificial Intelligence." Accessed June 3, 2025. https://www
.oed.com/.

Paradis, Tim. "Some Workers Are Warming Up to AI and Think It Will Help Their
Career," *Business Insider*, December 10, 2024, https://www.businessinsider.com
/workers-see-ai-automation-increasing-productivity-job-flexibility-2024-12?utm
_source=chatgpt.com.

Pazzanese, Christina. "Great Promise but Potential for Peril," *The Harvard Gazette*,
October 26, 2020, https://news.harvard.edu/gazette/story/2020/10/ethical
-concerns-mount-as-ai-takes-bigger-decision-making-role/.

Pellerin, Cheryl. "Project Maven to Deploy Computer Algorithms to War Zone by
Year's End," DOD News, July 21, 2017, https://www.defense.gov/News/News
-Stories/Article/Article/1254719/project-maven-to-deploy-computer-algorithms-to
-war-zone-by-years-end/.

People Power Family. "Don't Worry About a Thing," 2023, https://www
.peoplepowerfamily.com.

Peters, B. Guy. "The Challenge of Policy Coordination," *Policy Design and Practice* 1
(2018): 1–11. https://www.researchgate.net/publication/324099292_The_challenge
_of_policy_coordination.

PICV ISA. "Cutting-edge Technology, the Essential Recycling Accelerator in Brazil,"
https://picvisa.com/cutting-edge-technology-the-essential-recycling-accelerator
-in-brazil/#:~:text=AUTOMATION%20WITH%20ARTIFICIAL%20INTELLIGENCE
%20AND,recoverable%20materials%20in%20plastic%20waste.

Power, Brad. "How to Get Employees to Stop Worrying and Love AI," *Harvard
Business Review*, January 25, 2018, https://hbr.org/2018/01/how-to-get-employees
-to-stop-worrying-and-love-ai.

PwC. "How Organizations Can Mitigate the Risks of AI," sponsor content from PwC,
in *Harvard Business Review*, December 20, 2021, https://hbr.org/sponsored/2021
/12/how-organizations-can-mitigate-the-risks-of-ai.

Qualtrix. "These State Governments Offer the Best Customer Service," May 23, 2024, https://www.qualtrics.com/news/these-state-governments-offer-the-best-customer-service/.

Rabasca Roepe, Lisa. "Think Computers Are Less Biased than People? Think Again," *Christian Science Monitor*, October 17, 2018, https://www.csmonitor.com/Technology/2018/1003/Think-computers-are-less-biased-than-people-Think-again.

Reflow. "City of Boston, Mayor's Office of New Urban Mechanics: New Urban Mechanics: Experimenting with Civic Engagement," accessed May 20, 2025, https://reflowproject.eu/best-practices/new-urban-mechanics-experimenting-with-civic-engagement/.

Rueter, Thad. "ClearGov Launches ChatGPT Tool for Municipal Budgets," *Government Technology*, March 7, 2023, https://www.govtech.com/biz/cleargov-launches-chatgpt-tool-for-municipal-budgets?utm_source=chatgpt.com.

Samuel, Sigal. "A New Study Finds a Potential Risk with Self-driving Cars: Failure to Detect Dark-Skinned Pedestrians," *Vox*, March 6, 2019, https://www.vox.com/future-perfect/2019/3/5/18251924/self-driving-car-racial-bias-study-autonomous-vehicle-dark-skin.

Sarkar, Arunima, et al. "Chatbots RESET Framework: Rwanda Artificial Intelligence (AI) Triage," World Economic Forum, March 31, 2022, https://www.weforum.org/reports/chatbots-reset-framework-rwanda-artificial-intelligence-ai-triage-pilot.

Schaake, Marietje, and Jack Clark. "Stanford Launches AI Audit Challenge," HAI Stanford, July 11, 2022, https://hai.stanford.edu/news/stanford-launches-ai-audit-challenge.

Sharkey, Catherine M., and Cade Mallett. "Artificial Intelligence for Retrospective Regulatory Review," *The Regulatory Review*, September 12, 2023, https://www.theregreview.org/2023/09/12/sharkey-mallett-artificial-intelligence-for-retrospective-regulatory-review/.

Shaw, Kate. "To Get Parole, Have Your Case Heard Right After Lunch," *Wired*, Apr 11, 2011, https://www.wired.com/2011/04/judges-mental-fatigue/.

Shirley, Chad. "The Status of the Highway Trust Fund: 2023 Update," Congressional Budget Office, October 18, 2023, 2, https://www.cbo.gov/system/files/2023-10/59634.pdf.

Shittu, Esther. "New AI Ethics Advisory Board Will Deal with Challenges," TechTarget, August 5, 2022, https://www.techtarget.com/searchenterpriseai/feature/New-AI-ethics-advisory-board-will-deal-with-challenges.

Simonite, Tom. "Algorithms Were Supposed to Fix the Bail System. They Haven't," *Wired*, February 19, 2020, https://www.wired.com/story/algorithms-supposed-fix-bail-system-they-havent/.

State of California. "State of California GenAI Guidelines for Public Sector Procurement, Uses and Training," March 2024, https://www.govops.ca.gov/wp-content/uploads/sites/11/2024/03/3.a-GenAI-Guidelines.pdf.

State of Tennessee. "Ensuring Likeness, Voice, and Image Security (ELVIS) Act,"
    2024, https://www.capitol.tn.gov/Bills/113/Bill/HB2091.pdf/.

Stern, Carly. "LA Thinks AI Could Help Decide Which Homeless People Get Scarce
    Housing—and Which Don't," *Vox*, December 27, 2024, https://www.vox.com/the
    -highlight/388372/housing-policy-los-angeles-homeless-ai?utm_source=chatgpt
    .com.

Susany, Brett. "Embracing AI's Transformative Power Has Massive Potential for
    Design and Construction," *Engineering News-Record*, October 3, 2024, https://
    www.enr.com/articles/59364-embracing-ais-transformative-power-has-massive
    -potential-for-design-and-construction.

Tableau. "Interactive Government Data Visualizations: Leading Through Change:
    COVID-19 Response Efforts," https://www.tableau.com/interactive-public-sector
    -gallery?utm_source=chatgpt.com.

Tech AI, the AI Hub at Georgia Tech. "Bringing AI to the World: Innovation,
    Collaboration, and Partnerships," Georgia Tech, https://tech.ai.gatech.edu/

United States Advisory Commission on Intergovernmental Relations. "Federally
    Induced Costs Affecting State and Local Governments" (M-193), September 1994,
    23, https://library.unt.edu/gpo/acir/Reports/information/m-193.pdf.

United States Cybersecurity and Infrastructure Security Agency (CISA). "Cybersecurity
    Incident & Vulnerability Response Playbooks," November 2021, https://www.cisa
    .gov/sites/default/files/2024-08/Federal_Government_Cybersecurity_Incident_and
    _Vulnerability_Response_Playbooks_508C.pdf?utm_source=chatgpt.com.

United States Department of Homeland Security. "Privacy Impact Assessment for the
    CBP Translate Application," March 16, 2021, https://www.dhs.gov/sites/default/
    files/publications/privacy-pia-cbp069-cbptranslateapplication-march2021.pdf/

United States Department of Homeland Security Privacy Office. "Privacy Incident
    Handling Guidance: DHS Instruction Guide 047-01-008," December 4, 2017,
    https://www.dhs.gov/sites/default/files/publications/047-01-008%20PIHG
    %20FINAL%2012-4-2017_0.pdf?utm_source=chatgpt.com.

US Government Accountability Office. *Artificial Intelligence: An Accountability
    Framework for Federal Agencies and Other Entities*, June 2021, https://www.gao
    .gov/assets/gao-21-519sp.pdf.

Veroke. "7 Key Considerations When Choosing A Cloud Service Provider," July 8,
    2024, https://www.veroke.com/7-key-considerations-when-choosing-a-cloud
    -service-provider/?utm_source=chatgpt.com.

Villali, John. "Advanced AI-Powered Energy Forecasting," IDC Research, Inc., July
    2023, https://www.sas.com/content/dam/SAS/documents/analyst-reports-papers/
    en/idc-advanced-ai-powered-energy-forecasting-113587.pdf.

Virtasant. "AI in Government Services Cuts Spending, Boosts Efficiency," *Enterprise
    AI Today* (blog), January 8, 2025, https://www.virtasant.com/ai-today/ai-in
    -government-services-efficiency?utm_source=chatgpt.com.

West, Darrell M. "What Is Artificial Intelligence?" Brookings Institution, October 4, 2018, https://www.brookings.edu/research/what-is-artificial-intelligence/.

The White House. "Executive Order on Advancing United States Leadership in Artificial Intelligence Infrastructure," January 14, 2025, https://bidenwhitehouse.archives.gov/briefing-room/presidential-actions/2025/01/14/executive-order-on-advancing-united-states-leadership-in-artificial-intelligence-infrastructure/.

The White House. "Memorandum on Advancing the United States' Leadership in Artificial Intelligence; Harnessing Artificial Intelligence to Fulfill National Security Objectives; and Fostering the Safety, Security, and Trustworthiness of Artificial Intelligence," October 24, 2024, https://bidenwhitehouse.archives.gov/briefing-room/presidential-actions/2024/10/24/memorandum-on-advancing-the-united-states-leadership-in-artificial-intelligence-harnessing-artificial-intelligence-to-fulfill-national-security-objectives-and-fostering-the-safety-security/.

The White House. "Memorandum on Preparing for and Responding to a Breach of Personally Identifiable Information," January 3, 2017, https://obamawhitehouse.archives.gov/sites/default/files/omb/memoranda/2017/m-17-12_0.pdf.

The White House. "President Donald J. Trump Takes Actions to Enhance America's AI Leadership," Fact Sheet, January 23, 2025, https://www.whitehouse.gov/fact-sheets/2025/01/fact-sheet-president-donald-j-trump-takes-action-to-enhance-americas-ai-leadership/.

The White House Office of Science and Technology Policy. *American Artificial Intelligence Initiative: Year One Annual Report*, February 2020, https://trumpwhitehouse.archives.gov/wp-content/uploads/2020/02/American-AI-Initiative-One-Year-Annual-Report.pdf.

World Economic Forum. "Chatbots RESET Framework: Rwanda Artificial Intelligence (AI) Triage Pilot," March 31, 2022, https://www.weforum.org/reports/chatbots-reset-framework-rwanda-artificial-intelligence-ai-triage-pilot.

World Economic Forum. "Responsible Use of Technology: The Microsoft Case Study," February 25, 2021, https://www.weforum.org/whitepapers/responsible-use-of-technology-the-microsoft-case-study/.

World Record Academy. "World's Largest Industrial Research Organization, IBM Research Sets World Record," November 26, 2024, https://www.worldrecordacademy.org/2024/11/worlds-largest-industrial-research-organization-ibm-research-sets-world-record-424467

Yarborough, Allison. "LILT Supports AI-Powered Translated Forecasts Offered by NOAA's National Weather Service," *LILT,* October 27, 2023, https://lilt.com/blog/lilt-supports-ai-powered-translated-forecasts-offered-by-noaas-national-weather-service.

Yawei, Li, and Liang Rui. "Local Governments, Hospitals in China Embrace DeepSeek," *Global Times*, February 23, 2025, https://www.globaltimes.cn/page/202502/1328947.shtml.

Notes

Introduction

1 "State of Ohio—Transforming Delivery of Health & Human Services through Robotics Process Automation," NASCIO Awards 2019, National Association of State Chief Information Officers, https://www.nascio.org/wp-content/uploads/2020/09/NASCIO-Awards-2019_State-of-OH-Bots.pdf.

2 "New Study Shows Substantial Potential of Artificial Intelligence for the Swiss Economy," Microsoft, October 3, 2024, https://news.microsoft.com/de-ch/2024/10/03/new-study-shows-substantial-potential-of-artificial-intelligence-for-the-swiss-economy/.

3 "AI Revolutionizes Ophthalmology with Oculomics for Cardiovascular Risk Assessment," News Medical, October 4, 2024, https://www.news-medical.net/news/20241004/AI-revolutionizes-ophthalmology-with-oculomics-for-cardiovascular-risk-assessment.aspx.

4 Brett Susany, "Embracing AI's Transformative Power Has Massive Potential for Design and Construction," *Engineering News-Record*, October 3, 2024, https://www.enr.com/articles/59364-embracing-ais-transformative-power-has-massive-potential-for-design-and-construction.

5 Christina Pazzanese, "Great Promise but Potential for Peril," *The Harvard Gazette*, October 26, 2020, https://news.harvard.edu/gazette/story/2020/10/ethical-concerns-mount-as-ai-takes-bigger-decision-making-role/.

6 Simon Ellery, "Fake Photos of Pope Francis in a Puffer Jacket Go Viral, Highlighting the Power and Peril of AI," CBS News, March 28, 2023, https://www.cbsnews.com/news/pope-francis-puffer-jacket-fake-photos-deepfake-power-peril-of-ai/.

7 John Hattie, Dylan Wiliam, and Arran Hamilton, "The Promise and Peril of AI: Will Machines Make Us More or Less Human?" The Educator Australia, August 31, 2023, https://www.theeducatoronline.com/k12/news/the-promise-and-peril-of-ai-will-machines-make-us-more-or-less-human/283150.

8 Mark Fagan, "AI for the People: Use Cases for Government," M-RCBG Faculty Working Paper Series 2024-02 (Mossavar-Rahmani Center for Business & Government, Harvard Kennedy School, August 2024), https://www.hks.harvard.edu/centers/mrcbg/publications/fwp/2024-02. See also Mark Fagan, "AI for the People: The Use of AI to Improve Government Performance," M-RCBG Faculty Working

Paper Series 2023-01 (Mossavar-Rahmani Center for Business & Government, Harvard Kennedy School, April 2023), https://www.hks.harvard.edu/centers/mrcbg/publications/fwp/2023-01.

Chapter 1

1 "These State Governments Offer the Best Customer Service," Qualtrix, May 23, 2024, https://www.qualtrics.com/news/these-state-governments-offer-the-best-customer-service/.

2 "Citizen Satisfaction With Federal Government Services Jumps Again, ACSI Data Show," American Customer Satisfaction Index, November 14, 2023, https://theacsi.org/news-and-resources/press-releases/2023/11/14/press-release-federal-government-report-2023/.

3 Sean Coffey, "Long Wait Times Create DMV Headaches; State Officials Say They Need More Employees," ABC 11, September 6, 2024, https://abc11.com/post/long-wait-times-create-dmv-headaches-state-officials-say-need-more-employees/15274897/.

4 Chad Shirley, "The Status of the Highway Trust Fund: 2023 Update," Congressional Budget Office, October 18, 2023, 2, https://www.cbo.gov/system/files/2023-10/59634.pdf.

5 Shirley, "The Status of the Highway Trust Fund," CBO, October 18, 2023, 3.

6 "Comparing the Compensation of Federal and Private-Sector Employees in 2022," Congressional Budget Office, April 2024, https://www.cbo.gov/publication/60235.

7 Monique Morrissey and Jennifer Sherer, "The Public-sector Pay Gap Is Widening. Unions Help Shrink It," Economic Policy Institute, August 29, 2024, https://www.epi.org/publication/widening-public-sector-pay-gap/#:~:text=Key%20findings,pandemic%20pay%20gap%20of%2013.9%25.

8 B. Guy Peters, "The Challenge of Policy Coordination," *Policy Design and Practice* 1 (2018): 1–11. https://www.researchgate.net/publication/324099292_The_challenge_of_policy_coordination.

9 Tom Christensen and Per Lægreid, "The Challenge of Coordination in Central Government Organizations: The Norwegian Case," *Public Organization Review*, 8, no. 2 (2008): 97–116, https://www.researchgate.net/publication/5153878_The_Challenge_of_Coordination_in_Central_Government_Organizations_The_Norwegian_Case.

10 "Federally Induced Costs Affecting State and Local Governments" (M-193), US Advisory Commission on Intergovernmental Relations, September 1994, 23, https://library.unt.edu/gpo/acir/Reports/information/m-193.pdf.

11 "Intergovernmental Relationships: Unfunded Mandates," OER Commons, https://oercommons.org/courseware/lesson/15206/student/?section=4.

12 "Intergovernmental Relationships: Unfunded Mandates," OER Common, 2.

13 "Intergovernmental Relationships: Unfunded Mandates," OER Common, 3.

14 James Broughel and Dustin Chambers, "Learning from State Regulatory Streamlining Efforts," National Governors Association, June 2022, 5, https://www.nga.org/wp-content/uploads/2022/07/State_Regulation_Report_June2022.pdf.

15 Broughel and Chambers, "Learning from State Regulatory Streamlining Efforts," National Governors Association, June 2022, 6.

16 Broughel and Chambers, "Learning from State Regulatory Streamlining Efforts," National Governors Association, June 2022, 6.

17 "Governor Hochul Signs Legislative Package to Support New York's Hospitality Industry," October 9, 2024, https://www.governor.ny.gov/news/governor-hochul-signs-legislative-package-support-new-yorks-hospitality-industry.

18 Kenneth Chan, "BC Government Unveils New Digital Building Permitting Tool for Cities to Use," *Daily Hive*, May 27 2024, https://dailyhive.com/vancouver/bc-building-permit-hub-digital-application-tool#.

19 "New Permitting Strategy Will Help Build Homes Faster," British Columbia News, January 16, 2023, https://news.gov.bc.ca/releases/2023WLRS0003-000033.

20 Tuition Benefits Program, New York & CSEA Partnership, https://nyscseapartnership.org/tuition-benefits.

21 Missouri Leadership Academy, https://leadershipacademy.mo.gov.

22 "City of Boston, Mayor's Office of New Urban Mechanics: New Urban Mechanics: Experimenting with Civic Engagement," Reflow, accessed May 20, 2025, https://reflowproject.eu/best-practices/new-urban-mechanics-experimenting-with-civic-engagement/.

23 City of Chicago, Department of Technology & Innovation, https://www.linkedin.com/company/city-of-chicago-dti/about/.

24 "How Chicago Is Improving Homeless Shelters Through Results-Driven Contracting," Bloomberg Philanthropies, 2023, https://whatworkscities.bloomberg.org/cities/chicago-illinois-usa/.

25 New Jersey Office of Innovation, "Impact Report 2024," https://innovation.nj.gov/impact-report/2024/about/.

26 Linda Malone, "Barely Touched by Human Hands: Automation Is Reshaping How USPS Serves You," *Postal Posts* (blog), United States Postal Service, December 19, 2023, https://uspsblog.com/usps-innovation-in-shipping-automation/#:~:text=Automation%20makes%20this%20work.,we%20call%20flats%20—%20every%20hour.

27 Malone, "Barely Touched by Human Hands," United States Postal Service, December 19, 2023.

Chapter 2

1 "City to Launch Project Requirements Exploration and eComply Digital Permitting Tools," City of Vancouver, June 13, 2023, https://vancouver.ca/news-calendar/city -to-launch-project-requirements-exploration-and-ecomply-digital-permitting-tools .aspx.

2 Matthew Hutson, "Even Artificial Intelligence Can Acquire Biases Against Race and Gender," *Science*, April 13, 2017, https://www.science.org/content/article/even -artificial-intelligence-can-acquire-biases-against-race-and-gender.

3 Catherine M. Sharkey and Cade Mallett, "Artificial Intelligence for Retrospective Regulatory Review," *The Regulatory Review*, September 12, 2023, https:// www.theregreview.org/2023/09/12/sharkey-mallett-artificial-intelligence-for -retrospective-regulatory-review/.

4 Arunima Sarkar et al., "Chatbots RESET Framework: Rwanda Artificial Intelligence (AI) Triage Pilot," World Economic Forum, March 31, 2022, https://www.weforum .org/reports/chatbots-reset-framework-rwanda-artificial-intelligence-ai-triage-pilot.

5 *Tax Administration 2019: Comparative Information on OECD and Other Advanced Emerging Economies* (OECD Publishing, 2019), https://read.oecd-ilibrary.org/ taxation/tax-administration-2019_74d162b6-en.

6 Cristina García-Herrera Blanco, "The Use of Artificial Intelligence by Tax Administrations, A Matter of Principles," *CIAT* (blog), Inter-American Center of Tax Administrations, March 2, 2020, https://www.ciat.org/the-use-of-artificial -intelligence-by-tax-administrations-a-matter-of-principles/?lang=en.

7 Jory Heckman, "IRS Expands AI-powered Bots to Set Up Payment Plans with Taxpayers over the Phone," Federal News Network, June 17, 2022, https:// federalnewsnetwork.com/artificial-intelligence/2022/06/irs-expands-ai-powered -bots-to-set-up-payment-plans-with-taxpayers-over-the-phone/.

8 Carly Stern, "LA Thinks AI Could Help Decide Which Homeless People Get Scarce Housing—and Which Don't," *Vox*, December 27, 2024, https://www.vox.com/the -highlight/388372/housing-policy-los-angeles-homeless-ai?utm_source=chatgpt .com.

9 Stern, "LA Thinks AI Could Help Decide . . ." *Vox*, December 27, 2024.

10 Stern, "LA Thinks AI Could Help Decide . . ." *Vox*, December 27, 2024.

11 Abby Hughes, "AI Is Helping Outreach Workers in L.A. Predict and Prevent Homelessness," CBC Radio, October 12, 2023, https://www.cbc.ca/radio /asithappens/ai-is-helping-outreach-workers-in-l-a-predict-and-prevent -homelessness-1.6993119.

12 Hughes, "AI Is Helping Outreach Workers in L.A. Predict . . ." CBC Radio, October 12, 2023.

13 Jessie O'Brien, "How Pinellas County Made Strategic Planning Simple," Polco, September 7, 2023, https://blog.polco.us/how-pinellas-county-made-strategic-planning-simple.

14 O'Brien, "How Pinellas County Made Strategic Planning Simple," Polco, September 7, 2023.

15 Miguel Eiras Antunes, "Surveillance and Predictive Policing Through AI," from *Urban Future with a Purpose*, Deloitte Insights, 2021, https://www.deloitte.com/an/en/Industries/government-public/perspectives/urban-future-with-a-purpose/surveillance-and-predictive-policing-through-ai.html.

16 Tom Simonite, "Algorithms Were Supposed to Fix the Bail System. They Haven't," *Wired*, February 19, 2020, https://www.wired.com/story/algorithms-supposed-fix-bail-system-they-havent/.

17 People Power Family, "Don't Worry About a Thing," 2023, https://www.peoplepowerfamily.com.

18 "Home Care," Care Predict, 2025, https://www.carepredict.com/home-care/.

19 Zoë Corbyn, "The Future of Elder Care Is Here—and It's Artificial Intelligence," *The Guardian*, June 3, 2021, https://www.theguardian.com/us-news/2021/jun/03/elder-care-artificial-intelligence-software.

20 Corbyn, "The Future of Elder Care Is Here . . ." *The Guardian*, June 3, 2021.

21 "ICE Extreme Vetting Initiative: A Resource Page," Brennan Center for Justice, Updated: May 24, 2018, https://www.brennancenter.org/our-work/research-reports/ice-extreme-vetting-initiative-resource-page.

22 James Hendler, "As Governments Adopt Artificial Intelligence, There's Little Oversight and Lots of Danger," Route Fifty, April 19, 2019, https://www.route-fifty.com/digital-government/2019/04/as-governments-adopt-artificial-intelligence-theres-little-oversight-and-lots-of-danger/298257/.

23 Hendler, "As Governments Adopt Artificial Intelligence . . . ," Route Fifty, April 19, 2019.

Chapter 3

1 Definition of "Artificial Intelligence," *Oxford English Dictionary*, https://www.oed.com/.

2 Entry on "Human Intelligence," *Britannica*, https://www.britannica.com/science/human-intelligence-psychology.

3 "Human Intelligence," *Britannica*, page 2 of 26.

4 Darrell M. West, "What Is Artificial Intelligence?" Brookings Institution, October 4, 2018, https://www.brookings.edu/research/what-is-artificial-intelligence/.

5 For a comprehensive description of the Turing test, see the *Britannica* entry on "Human Intelligence," page 10 of 26.

6   "Human Intelligence," *Britannica*, page 2 of 26.

7   "Human Intelligence," *Britannica*, page 2 of 26.

Chapter 4

1   Jeffrey Dastin, "Amazon Scraps Secret AI Recruiting Tool that Showed Bias Against Women," Reuters, October 10, 2018, https://www.reuters.com/article/world/ insight-amazon-scraps-secret-ai-recruiting-tool-that-showed-bias-against-women -idUSKCN1MK0AG/.

2   Jordan Ellenberg, "Abraham Wald and the Missing Bullet Holes," Medium, July 14, 2016, https://medium.com/@penguinpress/an-excerpt-from-how-not-to-be-wrong -by-jordan-ellenberg-664e708cfc3d.

3   Lori Andrews and Hannah Bucher, "Automating Discrimination: AI Hiring Practices and Gender Inequality," *Cardoz Law Review*, 44, no. 1 (October 2022), https:// cardozolawreview.com/automating-discrimination-ai-hiring-practices-and-gender -inequality/.

4   Will Douglas Heaven, "Predictive Policing Algorithms Are Racist. They Need to Be Dismantled," *MIT Technology Review*, July 17, 2020, https://www.technologyreview .com/2020/07/17/1005396/predictive-policing-algorithms-racist-dismantled -machine-learning-bias-criminal-justice/.

5   Sigal Samuel, "A New Study Finds a Potential Risk with Self-driving Cars: Failure to Detect Dark-skinned Pedestrians," *Vox*, March 6, 2019, https://www.vox.com/future -perfect/2019/3/5/18251924/self-driving-car-racial-bias-study-autonomous-vehicle -dark-skin.

6   New York City, "The New York City Artificial Intelligence Action Plan," October 2023, https://www.nyc.gov/assets/oti/downloads/pdf/reports/artificial-intelligence-action -plan.pdf.

7   Xinyue Li et al., "Bias Behind the Wheel: Fairness Testing of Autonomous Driving Systems," *ACM Transactions on Software Engineering and Methodology*, 1, no. 1 (July 2024), https://arxiv.org/pdf/2308.02935.

8   Molly Bohannon, "Lawyer Used ChatGPT In Court—And Cited Fake Cases. A Judge Is Considering Sanctions," *Forbes*, June 8, 2023, https://www.forbes.com /sites/mollybohannon/2023/06/08/lawyer-used-chatgpt-in-court-and-cited-fake -cases-a-judge-is-considering-sanctions/.

9   "How Organizations Can Mitigate the Risks of AI," sponsor content from PwC, in *Harvard Business Review*, December 20, 2021, https://hbr.org/sponsored/2021/12 /how-organizations-can-mitigate-the-risks-of-ai.

10 Cindy Gordon, "2022: The Year of AI Hopes and Horrors," *Forbes*, December 30, 2022, https://www.forbes.com/sites/cindygordon/2022/12/30/ai-hopes-and -horrors/.

11 "MIT Work of the Future," MIT Industrial Performance Center, https://workofthefuture
    .mit.edu/research-post/artificial-intelligence-and-the-future-of-work/.

12 Recommendation of the Council on Artificial Intelligence, OECD, May 3, 2024,
    https://legalinstruments.oecd.org/en/instruments/oecd-legal-0449.

13 *American Artificial Intelligence Initiative: Year One Annual Report*, The White House
    Office of Science and Technology Policy, February 2020, https://trumpwhitehouse
    .archives.gov/wp-content/uploads/2020/02/American-AI-Initiative-One-Year
    -Annual-Report.pdf.

14 "Promoting the Use of Trustworthy Artificial Intelligence in the Federal Government,"
    Federal Register, 85, no. 236 (December 8, 2020), https://www.federalregister.gov
    /documents/2020/12/08/2020-27065/promoting-the-use-of-trustworthy-artificial
    -intelligence-in-the-federal-government.

15 "President Donald J. Trump Takes Actions to Enhance America's AI Leadership,"
    Fact Sheet, The White House, January 23, 2025, https://www.whitehouse.gov/fact
    -sheets/2025/01/fact-sheet-president-donald-j-trump-takes-action-to-enhance
    -americas-ai-leadership/.

16 Reid Blackman, "Why You Need an AI Ethics Committee," *Harvard Business
    Review*, July–August 2022, https://hbr.org/2022/07/why-you-need-an-ai-ethics
    -committee.

17 "Responsible Use of Technology: The Microsoft Case Study," World Economic
    Forum, February 25, 2021, https://www.weforum.org/whitepapers/responsible-use
    -of-technology-the-microsoft-case-study/.

18 Esther Shittu, "New AI Ethics Advisory Board Will Deal with Challenges," TechTarget,
    August 5, 2022, https://www.techtarget.com/searchenterpriseai/feature/New-AI
    -ethics-advisory-board-will-deal-with-challenges.

19 Shittu, "New AI Ethics Advisory Board . . ." TechTarget, August 5, 2022.

20 Marietje Schaake and Jack Clark, "Stanford Launches AI Audit Challenge," HAI
    Stanford, July 11, 2022, https://hai.stanford.edu/news/stanford-launches-ai-audit
    -challenge.

21 Mai-Ann Nguyen and Philip McKeown, "5 AI Auditing Frameworks to Encourage
    Accountability," AuditBoard, October 17, 2024, https://www.auditboard.com/blog/
    ai-auditing-frameworks/.

22 *Artificial Intelligence: An Accountability Framework for Federal Agencies and Other
    Entities*, US Government Accountability Office, June 2021, https://www.gao.gov/
    assets/gao-21-519sp.pdf.

23 Ellen P. Goodman and Julia Tréhu, "AI Audit-Washing and Accountability," German
    Marshall Fund of the United States (GMF), November 15, 2022, https://www.gmfus
    .org/news/ai-audit-washing-and-accountability.

24 Artificial Intelligence Fundamentals Certificate, ISACA, https://www.isaca.org/
    credentialing/artificial-intelligence-fundamentals-certificate.

25 "Auditing Artificial Intelligence," ISACA, https://store.isaca.org/s/store#/store/browse/detail/a2S4w000004KoGpEAK.

Chapter 5

1 "New York State Will Monitor Its Use of AI After Signing New Bill into Law," CBC, December 27, 2024, https://www.cbc.ca/news/world/new-york-ai-law-1.7419529.

2 "Enterprise Use and Development of Generative Artificial Intelligence Policy," Massachusetts Executive Office of Technology Services and Security Enterprise Privacy Office, January 31, 2025, https://www.mass.gov/doc/enterprise-use-and-development-of-generative-artificial-intelligence-policy/download.

3 "OTI Announces Progress on Nation's First Comprehensive Artificial Intelligence Action Plan," New York City Office of Technology and Innovation, March 7, 2024, https://www.nyc.gov/content/oti/pages/press-releases/oti-announces-progress-on-nations-first-comprehensive-artificial-intelligence-action-plan.

4 "Information Technology Department Generative AI Guidelines," City of San Jose, September 23, 2023, https://www.sanjoseca.gov/your-government/departments-offices/information-technology/itd-generative-ai-guideline.

5 "Safe, Secure, and Trustworthy Development and Use of Artificial Intelligence," *Federal Register*, 88, no. 210 (November 1, 2023), https://www.federalregister.gov/documents/2023/11/01/2023-24283/safe-secure-and-trustworthy-development-and-use-of-artificial-intelligence.

6 "Memorandum on Advancing the United States' Leadership in Artificial Intelligence; Harnessing Artificial Intelligence to Fulfill National Security Objectives; and Fostering the Safety, Security, and Trustworthiness of Artificial Intelligence," The White House, October 24, 2024, https://bidenwhitehouse.archives.gov/briefing-room/presidential-actions/2024/10/24/memorandum-on-advancing-the-united-states-leadership-in-artificial-intelligence-harnessing-artificial-intelligence-to-fulfill-national-security-objectives-and-fostering-the-safety-security/.

7 "Executive Order on Advancing United States Leadership in Artificial Intelligence Infrastructure," The White House, January 14, 2025, https://bidenwhitehouse.archives.gov/briefing-room/presidential-actions/2025/01/14/executive-order-on-advancing-united-states-leadership-in-artificial-intelligence-infrastructure/.

8 Matt O'Brien and Sarah Parvini, "Trump Signs Executive Order on Developing Artificial Intelligence 'Free from Ideological Bias,'" Associated Press, January 23, 2025, https://apnews.com/article/trump-ai-artificial-intelligence-executive-order-eef1e5b9bec861eaf9b36217d547929c.

9 O'Brien and Parvini, "Trump Signs Executive Order on Developing Artificial Intelligence . . ." Associated Press, January 23, 2025.

10 Hope Anderson, Iesha Nunes, and John Oltean, "Newly Passed Colorado AI Act Will Impose Obligations on Developers and Deployers of High-risk AI Systems," White & Case, June 20, 2024, https://www.whitecase.com/insight-alert/newly -passed-colorado-ai-act-will-impose-obligations-developers-and-deployers-high.

11 "Ensuring Likeness, Voice, and Image Security (ELVIS) Act," Tennessee, 2024, https://www.capitol.tn.gov/Bills/113/Bill/HB2091.pdf/

12 Law on Automated Employment Decision Tools, New York City Council, 2021, https://legistar.council.nyc.gov/LegislationDetail.aspx?ID=4344524&GUID =B051915D-A9AC-451E-81F8-6596032FA3F9.

13 "State of California GenAI Guidelines for Public Sector Procurement, Uses and Training," March 2024, https://www.govops.ca.gov/wp-content/uploads/sites/11 /2024/03/3.a-GenAI-Guidelines.pdf.

14 "State of California GenAI Guidelines," March 2024, 7.

15 "State of California GenAI Guidelines," March 2024, 9.

16 Created following the example of the EU AI Act, OECD AI Principles, and White House AI Bill of Rights.

17 "Cybersecurity Incident & Vulnerability Response Playbooks," US Cybersecurity and Infrastructure Security Agency (CISA), November 2021, https://www.cisa.gov /sites/default/files/2024-08/Federal_Government_Cybersecurity_Incident_and _Vulnerability_Response_Playbooks_508C.pdf?utm_source=chatgpt.com.

18 "Memorandum on Preparing for and Responding to a Breach of Personally Identifiable Information," The White House, January 3, 2017, https:// obamawhitehouse.archives.gov/sites/default/files/omb/memoranda/2017/m-17 -12_0.pdf.

19 "Privacy Incident Handling Guidance: DHS Instruction Guide 047-01-008," US Department of Homeland Security Privacy Office, December 4, 2017, https://www .dhs.gov/sites/default/files/publications/047-01-008%20PIHG%20FINAL%2012-4 -2017_0.pdf?utm_source=chatgpt.com.

Chapter 6

1 Ágnes Fekete, "Data Anonymization Tools: The 4 Best and the 7 Worst Choices for Privacy," Mostly AI, September 28, 2023, https://mostly.ai/blog/data-anonymization -tools.

2 Foundations for Evidence-Based Policymaking Act of 2018, Pub. L. No. 115–435, 132 Stat. 5529 (2019), https://www.congress.gov/115/plaws/publ435/PLAW -115publ435.pdf.

3 "LOCK IT. Protect the Information that You Keep," in *Protecting Personal Information: A Guide for Business*, Federal Trade Commission, October 2016, https://www

.ftc.gov/business-guidance/resources/protecting-personal-information-guide -business#LockIt.

4 US State Privacy Legislation Tracker, International Association of Privacy Professionals (IAPP), Updated: 7 April 2025, https://iapp.org/resources/article/us -state-privacy-legislation-tracker/.

5 Jim O'Reilly, "Choosing a Cloud Provider: 8 Storage Considerations," Network Computing, September 13, 2017, https://www.networkcomputing.com/cloud -networking/choosing-a-cloud-provider-8-storage-considerations?utm_source =chatgpt.com.

6 O'Reilly, "Choosing a Cloud Provider," Network Computing, September 13, 2017.

7 O'Reilly, "Choosing a Cloud Provider," Network Computing, September 13, 2017.

8 "7 Key Considerations When Choosing A Cloud Service Provider," Veroke, July 8, 2024, https://www.veroke.com/7-key-considerations-when-choosing-a-cloud -service-provider/?utm_source=chatgpt.com.

9 "7 Key Considerations When Choosing A Cloud Service Provider," Veroke, July 8, 2024.

10 NIH Cloud Lab for AWS, National Institutes for Health STRIDES Initiative, https:// cloud.nih.gov/resources/cloudlab/aws-jumpstart/?utm_source=chatgpt.com.

11 Andrea Fox, "AI's Value Is Not Yet Clear in Benefits Administration, Says VA," Healthcare IT News, May 31, 2024, https://www.healthcareitnews.com/news/ais -value-not-yet-clear-benefits-administration-says-va?utm_source=chatgpt.com.

12 J. Lee et al., "BioBERT: A Pre-trained Biomedical Language Representation Model for Biomedical Text Mining," *Bioinformatics*, 36, no. 4 (February 15, 2020): 1234–40, https://pmc.ncbi.nlm.nih.gov/articles/PMC7703786/.

13 Cheryl Pellerin, "Project Maven to Deploy Computer Algorithms to War Zone by Year's End," DOD News, July 21, 2017, https://www.defense.gov/News/News -Stories/Article/Article/1254719/project-maven-to-deploy-computer-algorithms-to -war-zone-by-years-end/.

14 "The Veterans Affair (VA) Electronic Health Record Modernization—Integration Office (EHRM-IO) Is in Search for Microsoft Power BI (Power BI) Custom Visualizations," GovTribe, June 2024, https://govtribe.com/opportunity/ federal-contract-opportunity/the-veterans-affair-va-electronic-health-record -modernization-integration-office-ehrm-io-is-in-search-for-microsoft-power-bi -power-bi-custom-visualizations-36c10b24q0520.

15 "Interactive Government Data Visualizations: Leading Through Change: COVID-19 Response Efforts," Tableau, https://www.tableau.com/interactive-public-sector -gallery?utm_source=chatgpt.com.

16 "Start with Security: A Guide for Business," Federal Trade Commission, August 2023, https://www.ftc.gov/business-guidance/resources/start-security-guide -business.

Chapter 7

1 Andrew Johnson, "The Endless Struggle to Clean Up Rio de Janeiro's Highly Polluted Guanabara Bay," Mongabay, August 1 2023, https://news.mongabay .com/2023/08/the-endless-struggle-to-clean-up-rio-de-janeiros-highly-polluted -guanabara-bay/#:~:text=Five%20centuries%20later%2C%20the%20bay,Planter %20of%20mangroves.

2 Ludovica Mulè, "Revolutionizing Waste Management: The Role of AI in Building Sustainable Practices," AI for Good, May 7, 2024, https://aiforgood.itu.int /revolutionizing-waste-management-the-role-of-ai-in-building-sustainable -practices/#:~:text=Lastly%2C%20AI%2Dpowered%20sensors%20integrated ,repair%20and%20recycling%20of%20materials.

3 "Cutting-edge Technology, the Essential Recycling Accelerator in Brazil," PICV ISA, https://picvisa.com/cutting-edge-technology-the-essential-recycling-accelerator -in-brazil/#:~:text=AUTOMATION%20WITH%20ARTIFICIAL%20INTELLIGENCE %20AND,recoverable%20materials%20in%20plastic%20waste.

4 Virtasant, "AI in Government Services Cuts Spending, Boosts Efficiency," *Enterprise AI Today* (blog), January 8, 2025, https://www.virtasant.com/ai-today/ai-in -government-services-efficiency?utm_source=chatgpt.com.

5 Nell Derick Debevoise, "The Third Critical Step in Problem Solving that Einstein Missed," *Forbes*, January 26, 2021, https://www.forbes.com/sites/nelldebevoise /2021/01/26/the-third-critical-step-in-problem-solving-that-einstein-missed/.

6 Sophia Fox-Sowell, "Cyberattacks on State and Local Governments Rose in 2023, Says CIS Report," StateScoop, January 30, 2024, https://statescoop.com/ ransomware-malware-cyberattacks-cis-report-2024/.

7 Ian Duncan, "Baltimore IT Director Who Was at Helm during Ransomware Attack and City's Recovery Is on Leave," *Baltimore Sun,* September 10, 2019, https:// www.baltimoresun.com/2019/09/10/baltimore-it-director-who-was-at-helm-during -ransomware-attack-and-citys-recovery-is-on-leave/.

8 Lisa Rabasca Roepe, "Think Computers Are Less Biased than People? Think Again," *Christian Science Monitor*, October 17, 2018, https://www.csmonitor.com /Technology/2018/1003/Think-computers-are-less-biased-than-people-Think -again.

9 "Mayor Adams Releases First-of-Its-Kind Plan For Responsible Artificial Intelligence Use In NYC Government," Office of the Mayor, New York City, October 16, 2023, https://www.nyc.gov/office-of-the-mayor/news/777-23/mayor-adams-releases-first -of-its-kind-plan-responsible-artificial-intelligence-use-nyc#/0.

10 "Artificial Intelligence 2024 Legislation," National Conference of State Legislatures, September 9, 2024, https://www.ncsl.org/technology-and-communication/artificial -intelligence-2024-legislation.

11 "President Biden Issues Executive Order on Safe, Secure, and Trustworthy Artificial Intelligence," National Archives, Biden White House, October 30, 2023, https://bidenwhitehouse.archives.gov/briefing-room/statements-releases/2023/10/30/fact-sheet-president-biden-issues-executive-order-on-safe-secure-and-trustworthy-artificial-intelligence/.

12 David A. Garvin and Lynne Levesque, "A Note on Scenario Planning." Harvard Business School Background Note 306-003, November 2005. (Revised July 2006), https://www.hbs.edu/faculty/Pages/item.aspx?num=32841.

13 Thad Rueter, "ClearGov Launches ChatGPT Tool for Municipal Budgets," Government Technology, March 7, 2023, https://www.govtech.com/biz/cleargov-launches-chatgpt-tool-for-municipal-budgets?utm_source=chatgpt.com.

14 Tech AI, the AI Hub at Georgia Tech, "Bringing AI to the World: Innovation, Collaboration, and Partnerships," Georgia Tech, https://tech.ai.gatech.edu/.

15 Government AI Coalition, City of San Jose, California, https://www.sanjoseca.gov/your-government/departments-offices/information-technology/ai-reviews-algorithm-register/govai-coalition.

Chapter 8

1 "World's Largest Industrial Research Organization, IBM Research Sets World Record," World Record Academy, November 26, 2024, https://www.worldrecordacademy.org/2024/11/worlds-largest-industrial-research-organization-ibm-research-sets-world-record-424467.

2 "AI Going to Save Time, Money for Grant Thornton Tax Team," *The Australian*, January 5, 2025, https://www.theaustralian.com.au/business/companies/accounting-firms-reveal-how-ai-has-changed-professional-services-and-given-staff-more-time/news-story/12684490bf788397f0dce75817ec64ef.

3 Tim Paradis, "Some Workers Are Warming Up to AI and Think It Will Help Their Career," *Business Insider*, December 10, 2024, https://www.businessinsider.com/workers-see-ai-automation-increasing-productivity-job-flexibility-2024-12?utm_source=chatgpt.com.

4 Brad Power, "How to Get Employees to Stop Worrying and Love AI," *Harvard Business Review*, January 25, 2018, https://hbr.org/2018/01/how-to-get-employees-to-stop-worrying-and-love-ai.

Chapter 9

1 Cristina García-Herrera Blanco, "The Use of Artificial Intelligence by Tax Administrations: A Matter of Principles," Inter-American Center of Tax Administrations, https://www.ciat.org/the-use-of-artificial-intelligence-by-tax-administrations-a-matter-of-principles/?lang=en.

2 "Chatbot Development Cost in 2024," Antino, March 3, 2024, https://www.antino
   .com/blog/chatbot-development-cost.

3 Cory Breaux and Emin Dinlersoz, "Only 3.8% of Businesses Use AI to Produce
   Goods and Services, Highest Use in Information Sector," United States Census
   Bureau, November 28, 2023, https://www.census.gov/library/stories/2023/11/
   businesses-use-ai.html.

4 Narita International Airport Corporation, "Digital Transformation: Automation and
   Labor Efficiency," https://www.narita-airport.jp/en/company/airport-operation/
   action/airnarita/automation/.

5 Arunima Sarkar et al., "Chatbots RESET Framework: Rwanda Artificial Intelligence
   (AI) Triage," World Economic Forum, March 31, 2022, https://www.weforum.org/
   reports/chatbots-reset-framework-rwanda-artificial-intelligence-ai-triage-pilot.

6 AI Use Case Inventory (link to download spreadsheet), "The Government Is Using
   AI to Better Serve the Public," https://ai.gov/ai-use-cases/.

7 "The Government Is Using AI to Better Serve the Public," United States, https://ai
   .gov/ai-use-cases/.

8 John Villali, "Advanced AI-Powered Energy Forecasting," IDC Research, Inc., July
   2023, https://www.sas.com/content/dam/SAS/documents/analyst-reports-papers/
   en/idc-advanced-ai-powered-energy-forecasting-113587.pdf.

9 Kate Shaw, "To Get Parole, Have Your Case Heard Right After Lunch," *Wired*, Apr
   11, 2011, https://www.wired.com/2011/04/judges-mental-fatigue/.

10 Keith Kirkpatrick, "It's Not the Algorithm, It's the Data," *Communications of the
    ACM*, 60, no. 2 (February 1, 2017): 21–3, https://cacm.acm.org/news/its-not-the
    -algorithm-its-the-data/.

11 Insight from Darryl Slabe, HKS Master in Public Administration candidate.

12 "The Government Is Using AI to Better Serve the Public," United States, https://ai
    .gov/ai-use-cases/.

13 Government AI Coalition, City of San Jose, https://www.sanjoseca.gov/your
    -government/departments-offices/information-technology/ai-reviews-algorithm
    -register/govai-coalition.

14 MindTitan, "AI Use Cases," https://mindtitan.com/resources/industry-use-cases/.

Chapter 10

1 United States Department of Homeland Security, "Privacy Impact Assessment for
   the CBP Translate Application," March 16, 2021, https://www.dhs.gov/sites/default/
   files/publications/privacy-pia-cbp069-cbptranslateapplication-march2021.pdf/.

2 Julia Edinger, "Translation AI Helps Bridge Language Barrier for Minnesota DVS,"
   Government Technology, September 28, 2023, https://www.govtech.com/artificial
   -intelligence/translation-ai-helps-bridge-language-barrier-for-minnesota-dvs.

Chapter 11

1 "Online Translations at the Touch of a Button," *Lernende Systeme*, https://www
.plattform-lernende-systeme.de/practical-exampels.html?AID=357&utm_source
=chatgpt.com.

2 Allison Yarborough, "LILT Supports AI-Powered Translated Forecasts Offered by
NOAA's National Weather Service," *LILT,* October 27, 2023, https://lilt.com/blog/
lilt-supports-ai-powered-translated-forecasts-offered-by-noaas-national-weather
-service.

3 "Multilingual Parent-Teacher Conference, Chinook Middle School. Bellevue, WA,"
Education Case Studies, *Microsoft*, Microsoft Education, https://www.microsoft
.com/en-us/translator/education/case-studies/?utm_source=chatgpt.com.

4 Li Yawei and Liang Rui, "Local Governments, Hospitals in China Embrace
DeepSeek," *Global Times*, February 23, 2025, https://www.globaltimes.cn/page
/202502/1328947.shtml.

5 Microsoft, *Transforming Public Sector Services Using Generative AI: Global Case
Studies* (Microsoft, February 2024), 6, https://wwps.microsoft.com/wp-content/
uploads/2024/02/Transforming-Public-Sector-Services-Generative-AI-Report.pdf.

6 Microsoft, *Transforming Public Sector Services*, 7.

7 Microsoft, Transforming Public Sector Services, 8.

8 Rebecca Heilweil, "ChatGPT, Meet DHSChat: Homeland Security Has a New
AI Bot," *FedScoop*, December 17, 2024, https://fedscoop.com/chatgpt-meet
-chatdhs-homeland-security-ai-bot/.

9 Heilweil, "ChatGPT, Meet DHSChat," *FedScoop*, December 17, 2024.

10 Weslan Hansen, "DHS Unveils AI Chatbot for Streamlining Internal Operations,"
MeriTalk, December 18, 2024, https://www.meritalk.com/articles/dhs-unveils-ai
-chatbot-for-streamlining-internal-operations/?utm_source=chatgpt.com.

Index

Note: References in *italic* refer to figures.

About the Authors

Mark Fagan is Lecturer in Public Policy at Harvard Kennedy School. Mr. Fagan teaches Operations Management, Systems Thinking and Supply Chain Management, and Policy Development in the degree program. In executive education programs, he chairs a program titled AI in Action, teaching participants how to identify and prioritize AI use cases. He also leads programs on using evidence for decision-making and introducing the entrepreneurial mindset into government organizations. He has written extensively about how to leverage AI and works with organizations to make the promise of AI a reality. He leads the School's Autonomous Vehicles Policy Initiative. Mark has consulted to management in the public and private sectors on strategy issues for more than thirty years and was a founding partner of Norbridge, Inc., a general management consulting firm.

Ben Gillies holds a master in city planning from MIT and a master in public policy from Harvard University. His work focused on the impact of AI-based self-driving vehicles on cities and how policymakers can respond to the changes in transportation patterns, needs, and demand that these new vehicles might bring about. He has co-authored policy documents for local and state officials on autonomous vehicles through the Taubman Center for State and Local Government at Harvard and has helped implement a number of policy scrums and analysis sessions to assist local stakeholders wanting to prepare their communities for the arrival of these vehicles. Ben is the co-founder of a coffee shop company in Winnipeg, Canada, which is using cutting-edge technology to develop a new food service business model. He is experimenting with AI to assist baristas in improving the customer service experience. He lives in Winnipeg when he is not deployed fighting wildfires in Canada.